THE INVISIBLE THREAD

THE INVISIBLE

A Portrait of Jewish American Women

INTERVIEWS **Diana Bletter**   PHOTOGRAPHS **Lori Grinker**

THREAD

THE JEWISH PUBLICATION SOCIETY   Philadelphia · Jerusalem

In honor of my mother, Gladys Katcher Bletter, and in loving memory of my father, Sydney Bletter (Shlomo ben Nachman z″l), for giving me the courage to question and the confidence to pursue my dreams.

    D. B.

To Jenny Anderson, Charlotte Grinker, and Pauline Rosenberg, who, each in her own way, gave me a feeling for different cultures; and to all the women in the book, who, by inviting me into their lives, helped me discover my own Jewish identity.

    L. G.

Text copyright © 1989 by Diana Bletter and Roundtable Press, Inc.
Photographs copyright © 1989 by Lori Grinker
Developed by Roundtable Press
First edition   All rights reserved
Manufactured in the United States of America

Library of Congress Cataloging in Publication Data
Bletter, Diana.
  The invisible thread: a portrait of Jewish American women / by
Diana Bletter and Lori Grinker.
    p. cm.
  ISBN 0-8276-0333-9. —ISBN 0-8276-0334-7 (pbk.)
  1. Women, Jewish—United States—Interviews. 2. Women, Jewish–
United States—Religious life. 3. Judaism—United States.
I. Grinker, Lori. II. Title.
HQ1173.B57   1989
305.4'862073—dc19   89-2096
                       CIP

Fourth cloth printing, 1995
Fifth paperback printing, 1995
Designed by Adrianne Onderdonk Dudden

Contents

INTRODUCTION   8

SOURCES

Inheritance   *Ida Kohlmeyer*   14

Risks   *Judy Nieto*   18

Contradictions   *Susannah Heschel*   22

Music   *Deborah Katchko-Zimmerman*   26

Label   *Rebecca Mintz*   30

Pioneer   *Shirley Novick*   34

Uniqueness   *Diana Saunders*   36

Ceremony   *Louie Elfant Asher*   38

Motherhood   *Nancy Hoffman*   42

Universality   *Carol Sue Rosin*   45

Family   *Wendy Drezek*   48

Evolution   *Laurie Weil Mandell*   50

Therapy   *Rachel Wahba*   54

Image   *Arleen Sorkin*   57

Wandering   *Victoria Gabayan*   60

Tradition   *Elizabeth Morjain*   63

Paradise   *Fanny Wald*   66

Second Generation   *Mickie Shuv-Ami*   70

Hope   *Tova Berger*   72

Roots   *Elinor Guggenheimer*   76

CONNECTIONS

Honor   *Arlene Mitchell*   80

Diaspora   *Ruthe Sinow*   84

Potential   *Sorah Weisman*   88

Tzedaka   *Beryl Levine*   92

Impact   *Susan Fisher*   95

Leadership   *Shoshana Cardin*   98

Strength   *Rusty Kanokogi*   102

Self-Reliance   *Pauline Bart*   104

Uncertainty   *Marsha Greene*   107

Congregation   *Jean Liedman*   110

Influence   *Madeleine Kunin*   112

Home   *Julie Hilton Danan*   114

Support   *Melanie Groner*   118

Allegiances   *Lynn Huberman*   122

Purpose   *Joy Holtzman*   125

Mitzvah   *Bernice Friedes*   128

Matchmaker   *Irene Nathan*   130

Divorce   *Khane Feygl Abraham*   133

Exodus   *Galina Nizhnikov*   138

Emancipation   *Rosetta Buggs*   142

Service   *Julie Schwartz*   144

Sanctuary   *Laurie Lemel*   148

DISCOVERIES

Choice   *Tammie Reiter*   152

Spark   *Sherry Manning*   155

Visibility   *Dvora Gordon*   157

Mainstream   *Melody Bowen*   160

Search   *Barb Lang*   164

Prayer   *Judith Kramer*   167

Irony   *Susan Seidelman*   170

Illumination   *Claire Mendelson Ciss*   174

Survival   *Irena Klepfisz*   178

Atonement   *Francine Gottfried*   181

Balance   *Jane Lurie*   184

Messenger   *Fayge Estulin*   187

Kaddish   *Phyllis Toback*   190

Midrash   *Suzanne Benton*   194

Talmud   *Judith Hauptman*   198

Renewal   *Pamela Steinberg*   202

Transformation   *Ketura Eshel*   208

Bat Mitzvah   *Pearl Kleinberger*   212

Rosh Hodesh   *Julie Greenberg*   215

Return   *Diana Bletter*   218

Journey   *Lori Grinker*   221

ACKNOWLEDGMENTS   224

Introduction

When Lori and I first met in 1983 to talk about possible projects that we could work on together, I mentioned that I was going to the *mikvah*. "The what?" she asked. She had never heard of the *mikvah*, and since I had recently become more observant, the ritual was still new to me. I told her that some women, including feminists, were going to the ritual bath to affirm the connection between their body's natural cycles and their spirituality. I also said that few people had written about the *mikvah* and even fewer had photographed it, especially from a woman's point of view. We decided to put together photo essays along with several oral histories about the *mikvah* and other Jewish rituals. We wanted to examine how women were reclaiming traditional Jewish practices as well as creating new rituals to meet their spiritual needs.

Our project took off. We were exploring uncharted territory. We found women who had embarked on new paths within Judaism—for example, women who put on *tallit* and *tefillin*, rituals traditionally observed by men. On the other end of the religious spectrum, we interviewed and photographed a Hasidic butcher who has very traditional ideas about women yet has been a pioneer for women's education. We also documented women who were inventing new rituals, such as celebrating Rosh Hodesh, the arrival of the new month, with other women. We explored how women balance what seem like two competing forces—change and tradition—as they combine feminism with Judaism.

We were excited about our work on many levels. First, it was a way for us to investigate our Jewish heritage from a female point of view. We also had the opportunity to meet with dynamic women who were having a personal and profound impact on the Jewish community. When we spoke with other Jewish women about the project, we found that they shared our enthusiasm. They were curious about the rituals, and, more importantly, they could relate to many of the other women's feelings and ideas. We sensed a connection among all kinds of Jewish women—whether they were ambivalent or observant—that we began to describe as an "invisible thread."

Hearing women's stories about their lives sparked a desire in other Jewish women to talk about their Jewishness. Some said that they don't observe rituals but feel that being Jewish influences their work and their lives in various ways. Film director Susan Seidelman, for example, relates that her Jewishness gives her an ironic view of the world. Vermont Governor Madeleine Kunin sees her Jewish experience as an important factor in her political career. Others, such as actress Arleen Sorkin, feel that being Jewish affects the way women view themselves as well as the way others see them. Lori and I realized that this vast range of experience and perspectives has never before been documented. We decided to expand the book to include Jewish women around the country, women talking openly and honestly about what being Jewish means to them.

Our next problem was to find more women to photograph and interview! We composed a questionnaire and sent it out to synagogues and Jewish community centers around the country. We made hundreds of telephone calls and played a game known as Jewish

Geography. For instance, a woman in Portland, Oregon, knew of a woman in Bluefield, West Virginia, who knew Melody Bowen, whose husband works on a farm there. Women from all over sent us back thought-provoking responses. They expressed an eagerness to talk about their links to Judaism and to make a connection with other Jewish women. We wanted to include a broad range of women, and so considered their interests, age, religious involvement, profession, economic class, and life experience. We chose subjects who we feel represent significant aspects of being a Jewish American woman.

After agonizing over whom to include in the book, we traveled around the country—from New Orleans, Louisiana, to Billings, Montana. (Unfortunately, we never made it to Alaska or Hawaii.) We interviewed and photographed all kinds of women: a veterinarian in Montgomery, Alabama, and the granddaughter of a black Jewish slave in New York; a Jew by choice and a Holocaust survivor and her daughter, who talked about how that kind of catastrophe is transmitted from one generation to the next. Everywhere we went, we asked difficult questions: How does Judaism influence your work and your life? How does being Jewish make you feel different from other Americans?

When we set out we weren't sure what we would find. We wanted to uncover the connection—the invisible thread—that linked women to Judaism and to one another. What surprised us from the start is that we ourselves felt this bond with all the women we met. Many welcomed us into their homes as though we were long-lost family members; they cooked us meals, put us up, and endured our many questions as well as many hours of photographing.

There was an immediate, unspoken understanding between us and our subjects. We traded hopes, ideas, sorrows, and laughter—of course, laughter. Whether living in the panhandle of Texas—what Judy Nieto calls "miles and miles of nothing but miles and miles"—or in the Midwest—which Pauline Bart refers to as "White Bread America"—our subjects shared the same quick wit.

Along with their sense of humor, we found a seriousness of purpose. As Rusty Kanokogi says, "Jews are not frivolous people," and these women are proof of that. Almost all stress the importance of family and education; many talk about how they are influenced by the Jewish concern for the poor and for those less fortunate, by the need to work for justice. Although many of the women may not observe Jewish rituals, they still adhere to a concept that seems quintessentially Jewish: People need to live up to their utmost potential. Some see this drive to succeed as a gift of Jewish history, a legacy of thousands of years of struggle for survival. The women set goals for themselves and pursue them in spite of difficulties—whether it's rising to a prominent position in the banking world or working toward an understanding of the needs of the deaf within the Jewish community.

These women have far-reaching, ambitious goals for themselves as well as for the society around them. The winner of the Mobilian of the Year Award and a Sanctuary worker in Texas might appear quite different, but they both share the Jewish goal of *tikkun olam*, repairing the world. Even an assimilated Jew such as Carol Sue Rosin, who had never heard of *tikkun olam* before becoming involved with this book, shares this urgency to work for a better world. Like many other women who feel estranged from traditional Judaism, Rosin is still tapped into the collec-

9

tive Jewish conscience that strives for personal and global redemption. Women attempt to achieve this redemption through art, politics, social action, or prayer.

Being part of the Jewish minority in America has not been easy for many of our subjects. Few talk of overt anti-Semitism. Rather, they describe a sense of "otherness," of feeling different from those around them. As a child of immigrants, Ida Kohlmeyer developed a sense of herself and her responsibility at an early age. Others needed a longer time to gain a positive feeling of self-identity. As pluralistic as America is, Christianity is still the norm in most of the country. In places with few Jews, the women often feel they have to defend their right to be Jewish, to remain different. As Laurie Weil Mandell says, "My children have just as much right to be here as anybody else."

If anti-Semitism can be said to exist still in the United States, it has taken on a new, more subtle form. It's no longer acceptable to denigrate Jews on the whole, but both non-Jews and Jews alike derogate Jewish women. Women across the country spoke about how the negative stereotypes of Jewish American women—the Jewish Mother and Jewish American Princess labels in particular—have affected their self-esteem. Some women's fears of being labeled a Jewish American Princess—and the materialism and selfishness that implies—have caused them to dress and even speak differently; others want to disassociate themselves so much from the negative image that they deny their Jewishness and turn away from Judaism completely. We hope that *The Invisible Thread* shows that Jewish American women are far different from the myths associated with them. There are countless women around the country who personify true Jewish values of *tzedaka*. These women have responded to the prophet Isaiah's charge "to do

well: relieve the oppressed, judge the fatherless, plead for the widow." When Jewish women speak for themselves and share who they are, they prove that the stereotypes about Jewish women are as distorted as they are dangerous.

As Jewish women move beyond the stereotypes, they affirm their own religious, ethnic, and cultural identities. They also explore how they define themselves as Americans and as Jews. Many seem to be forging a daring Jewish American identity that will blend the best of American ideals—pluralism, equality, and freedom—with the best of Jewish values—tradition, history, and justice. Some Jewish women choose to set themselves apart from other Americans; others want to blend in; still others try to maintain a link to Judaism while participating in secular society. Elinor Guggenheimer maintains that although she fully participates in American life, it is her Jewish identity that gives her a true sense of belonging, while Lynn Huberman expresses a dual allegiance. Several women express the concern that becoming like other Americans could lead to forgetfulness. Dvora Gordon, for example, fights *against* the assimilation her parents fought *for*; but Barb Lang feels uncertain as she attempts to find a core of Jewishness that was somehow lost between generations.

Being Jewish in America offers a challenge to these women. As they rework their self-images, they also redefine their roles within the Jewish religion. Some of the women included here are in the forefront of an exciting movement. They are "empowering" themselves, as Julie Greenberg says, to create rituals that flow out of Jewish tradition and still have meaning for them as modern American women. Some of the rituals take new forms, such as Suzanne Benton's Mask Ritual Tales, in which she uses masks to tell stories from the Bible. Others are new twists on ancient rites, such as Phyllis Toback saying *kaddish* for her father. These activities show that Judaism itself is not a monolithic structure; rather, it is an organic community comprised of individuals who, in a sense, all weave a pattern into the religion's rich tapestry.

For many of these women, the balance between Judaism and feminism—what Susannah Heschel calls the struggle of Judaism with modernity—is not free of ambiguities. Some, like Judith Kramer, have come to terms with observances such as the prayer that Orthodox men say thanking God for not making them women. Others, like Talmud scholar Judith Hauptman, argue that it is not the time for women to reconcile themselves to past customs; rather, women now should study Jewish laws and texts to guide the community toward egalitarianism.

These women are having a deep influence on American Judaism. They are finding new recognition and blazing new paths; they are opening up Judaism to a creative fluidity. If Jews are required to be "a light unto the nations," then women are a light unto the Jews. As they blend Judaism with their personal visions, they expand the Jewish community to include others who feel disenfranchised or excluded. Their commitment, ideas, and dreams stretch Judaism so that it continues to evolve and embrace all Jews.

The women in this volume approach their Jewish identity in a multitude of ways. Each has a sense of what Judaism is and what it means to her. Yet their voices overlap; sometimes they echo one another. As each woman explores questions of family and relationships, of observances and actions, of the conflicts in her life and her understanding of the role Judaism plays, many issues emerge. We have decided to divide the interviews in this book into three salient motifs: the *sources* that give women their sense of Jewishness, the women's *connections* to their communities, and their *discoveries* about their Jewish identity and religious expression. Often, the women talk about all three ideas, entwining themselves in the fabric of Judaism once again.

Judaism provokes a plethora of definitions. Some conclude that Judaism is a culture, an ethnic group, even a state of mind; or, as Nancy Hoffman says, "something I feel in my bones." While they might disagree with one another's viewpoints about what being Jewish means (when you ask two Jews a question, you get three opinions), they are committed to their concepts of what the Jewish heritage means. Their struggles and contributions keep Judaism flourishing in America. Their connection to Judaism—in all its manifestations—is the invisible thread that joins Jewish American women everywhere.

Every Jewish woman has a thread that binds her to her Jewish heritage. For some, this thread is woven from a familial source: for instance, the example set forth by a mother or father. Others find that the core of their Jewishness comes from what they've lived through in later life. These experiences affect women's priorities, their hopes and commitments. Their Jewishness plays a role in shaping their self-images and their interactions with others. As women interpret Judaism for themselves, they translate the Jewish message and pass it on to those around them as well as to their sons and daughters—the next generation.

SOURCES

Inheritance

I am a first-generation American. My parents came from Bialystok, in what is now Poland. My mother was the backbone of the family: She was a far better businessman than my father, and she was very ambitious.

Mama had high aspirations for her children. I was a good high school student—as well as the only Jewish cheerleader—and she was very proud of that. She wanted her children to do the right thing. My brother, who was twelve years older than me, often told her, "You should do this, it's what Americans do," and she followed his advice. She wanted to maintain her Jewish identity, but she also wanted to be someone else—a very American woman.

I adored my mother, but, I'm ashamed to admit even now, she did embarrass me at times. She had Eastern European taste, manners, and clothing, and she never lost her accent. While I was studying for my college entrance exams, Mama was learning to read and write.

My strongest feelings of guilt and love are for my mother. That dual emotion for an immigrant parent is not unique. Thousands of immigrants' children must have felt this way. But my mother stuck out in New Orleans more than she might have in a northern city because there were so few immigrants like her.

Most of the Jews who were living in New Orleans when my mother arrived had come from Germany a long time ago. They had lived in the city for generations. These old-line Jews looked down upon Mama as though she were inferior. Some of my husband's relatives, for example, had trouble accepting me into their family because of who my parents were. They thought I was beneath them, even though I fit in with the "right" circle: I played mah-jongg and golf and did everything that well-to-do young women do.

World War II sobered me. Suddenly life became very precious and I realized it would be a sin to waste it. I decided to go to art school, and gradually I began to find myself and my individuaiity. The second part of my life began.

The spirit of my art is Jewish. My art reveals typically Jewish characteristics—searching for an individual identity, being emotional, expressive, forthright, stubbornly myself, and not hiding who I am. Perhaps being Jewish has made it easier for me to be an artist.

But the subject matter of my art is not Jewish at all. My work is influenced by art I've seen around the world and by the environment here in New Orleans. I'm especially inspired by the masks, colors, and costumes of Mardi Gras, even though Mardi Gras itself is a Christian holiday.

There is a great deal of intermingling among Jews and non-Jews in New Orleans, but a certain separation occurs at Mardi Gras time. Jews are never included in any of the Mardi Gras events. Some Jews leave town during Mardi Gras to avoid feeling rejected. But I won't do that—I love the street festivities. Still, the fact that Jews are excluded from Mardi

My mother often told me stories about her life in Europe. I still get goosebumps when I hear the word 'pogrom.' She'd begin her tales, 'In the middle of the night . . .' and then talk about horses and barbarians storming into people's homes. Her fear and anger penetrated me so deeply that I almost feel as if I experienced the pogroms, too.

Gras balls and clubs bothers me on principle. I probably feel this discrimination more deeply because of my mother.

Whenever I speak in public, I make sure to mention my Jewishness in one way or another. People see me as a successful American painter—I want them to know that I am Jewish. And I never realized why until just now: I'm trying to win battles for my mother. I'm still trying to prove she was as good as any other American.

I don't know how I fulfill myself as a Jew beyond that, however. I believe in the Ten Commandments, I believe that we should be forgiving and just, and that we should use our abilities to the utmost. But I wish my mother had taught me more about Judaism. Mama told me about the pogroms she lived through, but I never talked about them with my daughters until they were both grown up. I missed out on a lot of what my mother could have taught me about being Jewish—my daughters have lost even more. I regret that now. It's a very great loss.

IDA KOHLMEYER
New Orleans, Louisiana

It would shock people who know me to find out that I feel, not necessarily uprooted, but not as solidly planted as I might like to feel. It's because I can still visualize the scenario I heard from my mother: In the middle of the night, gangsters could burst in here and, out of sheer stupidity, break everything and even kill us. That's crazy, isn't it? I've lived in this house for forty years and in New Orleans for seventy-four years. You would think that I'd feel pretty cemented here. But I sometimes think these things.

Risks

My Jewish lines come through the men in my family. My grandfather—my father's father—married a non-Jewish woman but they raised my father as a Jew. Although my grandmother never converted, she's buried in the Jewish cemetery in Dallas, right next to my grandfather.

My mother was raised as a Christian. She and my father never talked about their religious differences until one summer when she sent my sister and me to vacation Bible school. My father came home that first night and heard us singing "Jesus Loves Me." He threw a fit. We never went back to Bible school. From then on, we were in temple every Friday night.

My mother formally converted to Judaism when I was thirteen. I never felt the need to convert since I wasn't baptized and was brought up as a Jew from an early age. I am Jewish because I believe in Judaism. I believe in the tenets of the religion. I don't care if Orthodox Jews say that only people born to Jewish mothers are Jews. Why should the Orthodox count as Jews only those people who are born to Jewish mothers, even if they don't know anything about the holidays or the prayers? And why should I be excluded when my religion is so important to me? The act of being born does not make a person a Jew. It doesn't matter who my parents are. What's important is that they raised me as a Jew; therefore, I'm a Jew.

Sometimes I feel like the man who was put in a concentration camp during World War II because his father was Jewish. When he tried to move to Israel

after the war, they told him he wasn't Jewish because his mother was Christian. He told them he'd find another country where he could live as a Jew, instead of Israel, where he couldn't.

Even though we're the only Jewish family in our county—that's 900 square miles—I love living in the Texas panhandle. People here have two distinct views of Jews. One image is of the Jew who lives in Israel, where he belongs. The second is the Jew who lives in America. He is that conniving trickster who will "Jew you out of" whatever he wants. People who know I'm Jewish still use that phrase in front of me—I want to smack them. Sometimes I don't say anything because most of the farmers who use that phrase are older than dirt. I could never change the way they think. Other times, I will say to someone, "I'm Jewish and I'm very proud of it and when you bad-mouth Jews as a whole, you're bad-mouthing me." That person might tell me, "I didn't mean you," but I'll say, "When you use the word Jew, I'm included. You didn't say, "All Jews except Judy."

If you're black, you never have to worry about letting someone know what you are—people know that as soon as they look at you. But when everybody seems to think you're the same as they are, sometimes it's very difficult to say, "Hey, wait a minute, I'm different." For example, I was asked by a farming magazine to write a diary about our daily life on the ranch. Three other women also wrote diaries, and they all mentioned their going to church on Easter Sunday. I didn't mention Passover, but I did say that I took my

When I was younger, I felt I was Texan first, American second, and Jewish third. When I grew up and traveled outside of Texas, I became an American first and a Jew second. Then, I had children and became a Jew first. My religion teaches my children right from wrong, decent from indecent, moral from immoral, and just from unjust.

children to the religious school forty-five miles away, in a different county, where I teach. The magazine editor simply assumed that I was Christian and changed my diary to say that we went to church and Sunday school.

It might be easier to say we are Jewish from the start, but I've seen too much prejudice to think that would help. A lot of people won't buy from us once they find out that we're Jews. That's ironic, since Arabs from overseas—who know we are Jews—will eat at our table and buy our grain. Other domestic businessmen won't deal with my husband because he's Mexican—

they think that the only thing Mexicans should do is pick cotton and grapes.

If someone asks me what I am, I never lie. But I'm not willing to take a financial risk and announce to the world, "My husband is Mexican and I'm a Jew." I'm concerned about being able to make enough money to put bread and butter in my children's mouths. Any day in my life I could choose not to live as a Jew to make our lives easier. But I've never been willing to make that choice.

JUDY NIETO
Vega, Texas

I'm used to being the only Jew wherever I go. It's like being the only Martian on the planet.

20

Contradictions

My experience as a Jew changed abruptly when I was about seven or eight. I was told that I could no longer sit next to my father at the synagogue and I could no longer kiss the hand of my uncle, the Kopicziniczer Rebbe—all because now I was a "big girl" and must stay with the women. From then on, I would stand in the doorway of the dining room and watch my uncle as he sat at a table surrounded by his Hasidim, while the women of the family bustled in the kitchen, preparing trays of food that they would leave at the door of the dining room. We weren't allowed to enter the room or to participate. Not only could the women not touch the rebbe; we couldn't even gather around and listen to his words and join in the singing.

It wasn't a matter of women being separate but equal. Being in the kitchen was in no way equivalent to being at the rebbe's *tish*—his table. It was clear to me even then where the importance was, where the holiness was. I resented it when I had to sit on the side with the women and watch the little boys go up to the *bimah* to open and close the *aron,* the ark, and follow the sefer Torah as it was carried around the synagogue.

Whenever I expressed my frustrations and anger at home, my parents supported me and told me I was right. My father was a professor of Jewish philosophy, and my mother is a musician. Judaism and a sense of holiness imbued our home—always in a gentle, loving way. My father always wanted me to lead the grace after meals—something that women traditionally don't do—because it was important to him that I be a full participant in Jewish religious life.

I was sent to a yeshiva as a child, and I discovered that the teachers didn't talk about the kinds of things my parents talked about—*why* we pray, for instance. They were more concerned that we had *davened* every morning and brought certificates signed by our parents to prove it. The biggest insult to me was that, while the boys were taught Torah for their bar mitzvahs, the girls were given sewing lessons in the library. I always got into trouble for sneaking a book off the shelf and reading instead of sewing.

The worst experience occurred when my father died and I wanted to say *kaddish,* the mourner's prayer, for him. I'm an only child and women are not supposed to say *kaddish.* So my male Hasidic cousins, as encouraging and supportive as they were of my intentions, said that they would take the obligation upon themselves—my *kaddish* didn't count. The real trouble began when I needed a daily *minyan.* Sometimes there would be nine men gathered—and me—and the *minyan* would be cancelled. Other times, I would stand to say *kaddish,* all alone, and the men would uncomfortably mumble a response. Once, when I was driving from Boston to New York, I stopped in New Haven for *minhah* services. I found the Orthodox synagogue where they had a daily *minyan,* but the services were held in a small classroom with no partition. One old man said, "We can't *daven* as long as you remain in the room." I told them that I had to say *kaddish,* and that I would stand in the back of the room or even in the hallway. But that made no difference; they told me I had to leave. So I left in tears, absolutely broken. It was the first time in my life that I really needed a Jewish community, and

I was once really fed up on *Simchat Torah.* I arrived at services with a male friend who had never even heard of the holiday even though he was Jewish. I had been going to this synagogue all my life, but the moment we arrived, *he* was given a *sefer Torah* to dance with while I had to stand in a corner with the women and watch. I was furious. But my father came over with a *sefer Torah* and danced with me. He could do that—no one would dare try to stop him! When my parents left a little early, I decided to be daring and join one of the groups of men dancing. One of them asked me, "Who gave you permission to dance here?" I answered, "God." They forced me out.

I expected to be received with warmth and love. I resented their rejection because I felt my father gave his life to the Jews of this country. His mission was to teach a theology of Jewish spirituality, of *ahavat Yisrael*—love and respect for other Jews.

Being a feminist—and I feel as though I was born a feminist!—gives me a different perspective. When I was a teenager, I used to argue with my parents' friends who taught at the Jewish Theological Seminary about women's participation in synagogue services. They said that a woman on the *bimah* would be distracting to men and that if women were counted in the *minyan*, men wouldn't come to synagogue any more. They quoted the Talmud, which prohibits women from reading from the Torah for the sake of the "honor of the congregation." I began to realize that the entire Jewish system is constructed as if the congregation were exclusively a congregation of men. What about women's honor, our religiosity, our spiritual needs and experiences? More and more I came to see that the issue of women in Judaism was not simple, and effecting change wouldn't come from modifying this or that point of Jewish law. Instead, I saw that the entire system excluded women's perspective.

I started reading the Torah differently. Even issues of religious philosophy, which I was studying in college, took on a new meaning. Why worry about the nature of God or revelation if the Bible itself teaches ideas and laws that deny women's humanity? For me, feminist questions are prior to those of philosophers. The critique of some Christian feminist theologians of the Bible, of Christian religious symbols and language, made me see similar problems in Judaism, in our exclusivist liturgy and some of the symbols evoked in certain Jewish observances. For instance, an association of male authority with divine authority emerges if only men stand at the head of the table at holidays and make *kiddush* or lead the *seder*.

Yet, I am still drawn to the Judaism that my father defined in his books and my parents created in our home. This is not the rigid, arbitrary religion I encountered in the yeshiva, nor as sexist and exclusivist as some feminist critics have portrayed it. I want to remain a committed Jew and a feminist, even though being both has often left me feeling tremendous pain and anger. While I have felt discouraged at times, the growth of a Jewish feminist community in this country has turned some of my anger into humor. I have a new community to talk to, people who understand my conflicts and support me. I think publishing my book, *On Being a Jewish Feminist,* and lecturing on the topic have helped me laugh instead of argue.

I'm also amazed by all the changes that have taken place in the last ten or fifteen years. I never thought, for instance, that the Jewish Theological Seminary would ordain female rabbis! Of course, that one change does not go far enough—many more fundamental changes for women are needed. I had once

considered going to the JTS rabbinical school, before they accepted women, but now I realize how difficult it would be for me—I'd always be questioning the curriculum, I'd argue about the texts we were studying. So perhaps it's better for me to be an academic—universities are more comfortable with critical analysis. Also, there are such marvelous women's studies programs flourishing in all fields at universities today that I feel very much at home and supported in my struggles.

My beliefs have put me in an interesting position—a little on the margins of both Judaism and feminism, always looking at things from other perspectives, always seeing tensions and ambiguities. My father used to say, "Show me a person who has no problems and I'll show you a fool." Too many Jews today want to solve everything, find simple solutions and answers—as if all we have are simple questions—when actually we have profound and exciting problems. I like the struggle and the conflicts. I don't want to live in a fool's paradise.

SUSANNAH HESCHEL
Philadelphia, Pennsylvania

Men have privilege in Jewish life, men have authority. I can never become a *rebbe*, but I have other things. I can see things that a man can't because I'm included and excluded at the same time. Having been born a woman gives me insight, and an understanding of Judaism that no man has.

Music

I grew up hearing my mother and father perform Jewish music throughout the year: He was a cantor, she was his organist. The music they played sounded so alive and natural that it resonated through the house. It was the most beautiful music I had ever heard; knowing that my grandfather had composed most of it made it even more special to me.

My grandfather was a cantorial prodigy in Europe during the 1930s—the golden age of cantorial music. Cantors were like Jewish rock stars in those days: People went to *shul* to hear a *hazzan* sing. When my grandfather came to America, he composed cantorial music, taught other cantors, and helped restructure the cantor's role in the synagogue.

Although I never thought I wanted to be a *hazzan* when I was growing up—I didn't know of any female cantors—I always enjoyed singing. I sang with a Jewish folk rock group in clubs and coffeehouses in Boston. When the Hillel director from Boston University heard me singing in a coffeehouse, he invited me to lead High Holiday services at the school that fall.

I experienced an overwhelming sense of spirituality the first time I sang *Kol Nidre* in front of two thousand people. Singing in that religious atmosphere inspired me much more than singing in a coffeehouse. I realized that cantorial music was in my blood—it felt like something I was destined to do.

I began singing as a cantor in Reform and Conservative synagogues in the Boston area. Although I liked the creativity of the Reform services, I felt more comfortable when I sang in Conservative synagogues.

Their respect for tradition was more in keeping with the fairly observant home in which I was raised. As soon as I heard of a full-time cantorial position in a Conservative *shul* in Connecticut, I applied, and was hired for the job.

When I first started working in the early 1980s, the Conservative movement was still struggling with the issue of whether women could be ordained by its seminary. At the time, there was only one other female cantor working in a Conservative synagogue. The question centered around the idea that a *hazzan* is considered the *shaliach tzibbur*, the messenger of prayer. If the *hazzan* represents the community before God, could a woman, who wasn't required to fulfill the same prayer obligations as men—such as praying three times a day and putting on *tallit* and *tefillin* each morning—act as messenger for the entire community? Yes, the Conservative movement leaders decided, if female cantors—as well as female rabbis—agreed to accept the same prayer obligations that men have accepted.

Some people feel that women shouldn't be cantors because men should not hear *kol ishah*, the voice of a woman. They argue that women's voices are sensuous, they distract men from prayers. This is an ancient custom—not a law—as well as an outdated way of thinking. Jewish men hear women's voices all the time, yet they go on with their work and their lives. I don't believe that a woman's voice would make a man lose his concentration. Permitting us to serve as cantors is a way to legitimize Jewish women and to show that we are just as focused and committed to prayer as men are.

A lot of people can sing opera beautifully, but to sing like a cantor is very different. There's a certain emotion that has to translate into the prayer that you can't get from perfect voice training alone. You have to grow with it; you have to hear the sounds so much in your head that you can recreate them.

I felt isolated during my first years as a cantor because I had no colleagues to share ideas with. The Conservative movement's Cantors Assembly is still an all-male body—even though female cantors have been ordained recently. That's why I decided to start the women's cantor network where I could meet with other female cantors to provide mutual support and learn from other women. I've found that female cantors experience different pressures than their male counterparts. We're all new in the field and we all need encouragement from one another. We also have extra stresses. Even though my husband shares household responsibilities equally with me, I still feel that the responsibility of child care arrangements rest mostly on me. When my congregation needs me at the same time my children are sick, my heart is torn. But I'm a professional and I have to do my job—I'm part of a tradition that has been passed from generation to generation, from my grandfather to my father to me.

When I was in college I studied with Elie Wiesel. He had a profound influence on my commitment to Judaism. As he explained, there are six million Jews in the United States—the same number of Jews who were killed in the Holocaust. If each Jew here took on the identity of a Jew who was lost, we would live not only for ourselves but for someone else as well. Our lives would be doubly meaningful. After he said this, I found out that my grandfather had three sisters and two brothers—both cantors—who were killed; there were twenty other singers in my family who perished. I thought about all the talented people whose lives were cut short, and I felt a strong sense of obligation. Suddenly it became clear to me that being a cantor is a way for me to fight against an enormous Jewish loss. Through my music, I'm keeping my family alive.

DEBORAH KATCHKO-ZIMMERMAN
Norwalk, Connecticut

The art of being a cantor was passed down from my grandfather to my father to me—and that isn't accessible to most Jewish girls growing up in America.

Label

People stereotype me as a "Jewish American Princess" when they find out that I live in Hewlett, Long Island. They look at my clothes, my jewelry, the car I drive. They assume that my parents give me a lot of money, that I get whatever I want, and that I'm haughty.

If I'm not labeled a "JAP," I'm called a "Daddy's girl." That implies that my father wants to keep me sheltered in an unreal world where he buys me whatever I want. But my father and I have a close relationship because we spend time together—he never takes me shopping. He also doesn't protect me from seeing the realities of life. I've traveled with him; I've seen poverty and problems, and I'm aware of how fortunate I am.

Some Jewish guys my age would say that I only want to go to college to get a husband. They assume that I'm incapable of getting a good job because I'm a girl. But things have changed since my mother went to school. I don't only want to marry. I want to study hard in college so that I can get a good job when I graduate. I might go into my father's business or do something completely different. I might even wind up being more successful than any of the guys in my class!

When I go on college interviews, I wear plain, pleated pants and a button-down shirt so that the interviewer won't judge me by my clothing and assume that just because I'm concerned with my appearance, I don't know how to think. When I attend college next year, I plan to dress conservatively. But I'm worried that even if I wear well-tailored, non-flashy clothes, people might still label me as a JAP. They might say it's the kind of socks I wear, or even the brand of sneakers. I'm nervous that when I walk into the dorm, my future roommate might look at me and think, "Oh, no, a Jewish girl from Long Island."

It isn't fair to stereotype all Jewish girls in this way. There are a lot of non-Jewish girls who are just as spoiled as Jewish girls. But people have preconceived notions about Jewish girls; we're given a very negative tag. If people met me with an open mind, they would realize that I don't walk around thinking I'm superior. My mother and father have tried hard to help me see right from wrong. They've taught me not to talk behind people's backs, not to manipulate people, not to lie. Honestly, I'm not a bad person.

When I have kids, I don't know if I should say, "You can have one new dress and that's it." Or would it be better to say, "We can afford it, so let's buy you two new dresses." I know my parents felt that since they had the money, they wanted to give me things—as long as I appreciated what I had. Maybe my parents could have been more strict with me, but if I were the only girl who didn't have a new Italian sweater, for example, I would have felt bad. My parents never wanted me to feel left out. But don't get me wrong—they don't give me everything I want. They won't give me a stereo for my room, for example. They feel that's a luxury and they want to show me that I can live without all these things.

Money isn't everything. I know kids who have more money than anyone could ever imagine, but their parents are getting divorced. I feel lucky that my mother and father live with me.

There's nothing wrong with people being well-off, as long as it doesn't limit how other people view them. That's why the "Jewish American Princess" label bothers me. It connects Judaism with money and turns the religion into a stereotype.

I want people to know that I'm Jewish—but not because of my material possessions. I am Jewish because I had a bat mitzvah. (Some people said the event was extravagant, but it was significant to me.)

Judaism means helping other Jews; it means celebrating holidays with my family, belonging to a temple, believing in Israel. I don't want to be connected to Judaism because I drive a car that other Jews might drive, or wear an outfit that other Jewish girls wear. People should label me as Jewish not because of what I have but because of what I believe.

REBECCA MINTZ
Hewlett, Long Island

When we go to temple on the High Holidays, the women are all decked out. My mother, sister, and I put on whatever we have, but some of these women dress as if they're in a fashion show. It doesn't turn me off from Judaism, though. It just makes me want to get a good seat in temple and watch.

Pioneer

I was a rank-and-file union member. I wasn't an official—they were mostly men—but I was an activist. It was my life's work for forty-seven years. Being in the union was the only way for me to fight for better conditions in the dressmaking sweatshops where we worked.

We had to fight for every nickel we earned. We even had to fight to have the floor swept—it was filthy with dust, lint, dirt—and to have the washrooms cleaned. Most of the bosses were Jewish men who knew nothing when they came to this country and worked their way up to the top. For some reason, I expected them to have high moral values. I used to shake them up at times: How can you allow such conditions to go on? They had their reasons—they claimed they had to compete against cheaper labor in the South—but we continued to struggle with them and the union bureaucracy for our daily bread and butter.

There were a lot of other Jewish women involved in the unions. After all, we were young immigrant girls who had nothing to lose. In general, I would say that Jews have played a very big part in union movements because we've always been an oppressed people. And the Jewish women who came here understood class struggle. We had read books, we understood politics, we were enlightened. I felt I had a responsibility to educate—if not agitate.

For instance, I worked in one shop where all the other women were Italians. They were more concerned with their family than with the union, and they were frightened of "il padrone." But I used to come in and sit by the machine and tell the women stories from Sholom Aleichem and other books I read. The women gradually put down their sewing to listen, so the boss would yell at me. Even though the other women never became involved in union activity, they learned a lot from me. They elected me to be their delegate to settle prices with our bosses.

Young Jewish women today are educated and have good jobs, but they didn't get there by themselves. Their mothers and grandmothers worked in sweatshops to send their daughters to college so that they could have better jobs. We fought for things that young Jewish women today—like other Americans—take for granted. No one should forget that we struggled for better working conditions for everyone.

Take Social Security, for example. I went to the first demonstration in support of Social Security and unemployment benefits on March 6, 1930, in Union Square. I'll never forget the date and the year because back then, Social Security and unemployment benefits were considered unattainable, the dream of crazy people. But I fought for it! If it weren't for the Social Security system today, millions of Americans would now be starving.

I've certainly given a lot to America. I've been fighting since I came here in 1928 from Poland. I never wanted to sit on the sidelines and do nothing. And there were tens of thousands of Jewish women like me. We helped shape the unions, we helped shape America. We were the pioneers! Only we didn't shape it well enough. I still want to see a better America and a better world.

SHIRLEY NOVICK
New York, New York

In 1947 I was sent by the women in my shop to Washington to canvass our representatives about establishing a state of Israel. I felt very proud. I had lost my whole family in the Holocaust, and I felt that after the destruction of six million of us, Jews needed a homeland.

Uniqueness

Most Jewish women bring up their daughters to cook, clean, and sew. But the only thing my mother taught me to sew was ribbons onto my ballet shoes. She always wanted to be a dancer but she never worked professionally because her father, an Orthodox Jew, thought only immoral women danced.

When I was a little girl, my mother played music and danced around the house. She was determined that one of her daughters would be a dancer, and by the time I was eleven I knew that dancing was my life's work. I don't think it's strange that I'm living out her fantasy; in fact, I'm grateful that she had that dream. Because of her I broke free from the traditional mold for Jewish women—to marry a nice Jewish doctor, take care of him, and raise a family.

There's nothing wrong with getting married and having children, but I wanted to do something more with my life. I've appeared on Broadway and in television specials; I've danced across the United States, in France and Australia, and I'm still working at my craft.

I've found job security here in Las Vegas. When I was working on Broadway, as soon as I landed a job, I had to go out and look for another one. A show might have closed at any moment. After twenty years of *shlepping* around to make ends meet, I feel lucky to have a job that's lasted five years. I finally have a house with a garden—something I never could have achieved if I had continued to work in New York.

In the dancing world, auditions are known as cattle calls. If a show requires eight dancers, two hundred show up for the audition. I've become strong because I've had to fight every day just to continue dancing. I'm no longer hurt by what people say to me, and I've learned how to distinguish myself in a crowd of dancers. In many ways, being a dancer parallels what it's like to be a Jew.

When I was first hired to dance here, I was a featured soloist. Now only women who dance topless are given solo parts. I don't put down topless dancers because many of them are my friends. They don't mix and mingle in bars—they take their children to church every Sunday.

But I don't dance topless because I don't have to prove my worth that way. I know I'm a good dancer. Like many other Jews, I was brought up to feel special. My mother never said, "Jews are better than Christians," but she did give me a sense of pride about our uniqueness. She pushed me to be the best, just as Jews have striven to be the best throughout history. As a Jew and as a dancer, I don't blend into the background. I may be one of the sixteen dancers on stage, but I still feel like I'm the only one out there.

DIANA SAUNDERS
Las Vegas, Nevada

I'm a coupon cutter. I once borrowed my friend's newspaper and when she looked at it later, she found a page missing. She joked, "Oh, the Jew's been at the paper." Her comment might have been based on the stereotype that a Jew can squeeze two dollars out of every one dollar, but she was teasing me with humor and love. I laughed with her, and ever since then, my closest friends call me "Jew" as a nickname. They bought me the towel with "Jew" embroidered on it. For me, it's a term of endearment.

Ceremony

I have always taken prayers seriously. When I was a little kid, I went to an area near my house where there had been a brush fire. I buried a twig in the ground and said a prayer over it. I made up my own ceremony. That was typical of my sensibilities; I had a quiet piety that was my own.

My family belonged to a small, new Conservative synagogue; the rabbi was an observant man who was also progressive. He placed a great emphasis on youth activities and the junior congregation. As a member of the junior congregation, I got to be rabbi and lead services, even learning to lead High Holiday prayers with their own special tunes and cadences. After my bat mitzvah, I was allowed to lead services in the main congregation. Nobody had any objections. If an older woman had been the first woman to have an *aliyah*, people might have felt it was too radical. But allowing the girls who had grown up in the congregation to be the first women to take on public functions was an easier way to introduce change. It was an evolutionary process. I took my role in the synagogue for granted—I didn't realize that I was doing things that few women had ever done—but it was still important for me.

Attending Camp Ramah when I was a teenager also shaped my early Jewish commitment. For the first time, I had the opportunity to be with people who not only took their religion seriously, but who really led Jewish lives under the auspices of the Conservative movement. A conflict arose, for instance, about whether the camp should have an all-star team. Some people said that we should—an all-star team is such an American ideal—but most of the camp leaders felt that it wasn't a Jewish concept. In an ideal Jewish community people are not excluded from any activity. The whole community has to learn to care for one another.

I was very excited. I came from a family that was committed to Judaism but that wasn't very knowledgeable or observant. Camp instilled in me a desire to learn and do more. Although my family wasn't kosher, I decided to become kosher on my sixteenth birthday. My camp friends became my friends for life. In fact, as a college freshman, I attended my first *havurah* (which basically means fellowship) service started by people who had also been at Ramah.

I loved those early *havurah* services. It was during the 1960s, and everyone sat in a circle on the floor, singing songs and being spiritual together. But it wasn't some form of Eastern meditation—it was Jewish! The leaders of the *havurah* were influenced by Hasidism, they wanted to celebrate Judaism joyously with song and dance.

In some ways, the *havurah* movement was a Jewish counterculture. It was anti-establishment, a reaction to the way typical American synagogues had become—too large and impersonal. In a *havurah*, everyone is supposed to lead and participate. A traditional prayer book is sometimes used, but often, whoever is leading services can innovate creatively and add personal meaning.

I'm involved with the *havurah* movement in Philadel-

My children live in such a Jewish environment that I wanted to give them a broader experience in the summer. So I enrolled them in a YMCA camp to meet children named Jimmy and Chris. But they didn't know anyone in the camp and they hated it. My six-year-old daughter explained, "Mommy, I feel more comfortable with Jewish people."

phia. The two groups I attend maintain Jewish rituals and take *halakhah*, Jewish law, seriously. Both conduct their services in Conservative synagogues. We no longer sit on the floor, but one group still sits in a semi-circle with everyone facing one another. The Torah is read from a central position, which gives a sense of immediacy. We all sing together and take turns giving the *d'var Torah*—comments on the weekly portion—sometimes with a discussion as well. We always welcome newcomers because it's a Jewish requirement to welcome strangers in your midst.

My husband and I invite people to come to Friday night services that we conduct in our home once a month. I often lead our services. My husband and I also ask other women to lead services, but there aren't many women who feel comfortable doing it—it's new for them.

Over fifteen years ago, I read the *megillah* at a *havurah* Purim service in Boston. I was the first woman to do so, and it was very dramatic. When women told me how impressed they were, I realized that I had become a role model: My reading the *megillah* encouraged other women to take on more public functions in Judaism.

I want my daughters to know that they can lead full Jewish lives in an active community without sitting behind a partition in an Orthodox synagogue. I want them to feel that it is natural for a woman to lead services. I hope that my example makes other women—as well as men—feel comfortable with women's participation in all aspects of Jewish life.

LOUIE ELFANT ASHER
Philadelphia, Pennsylvania

I'm very moved by the Tisha b'Av reading of the Book of Lamentations. The images of the devastation upon the women of Jerusalem are especially powerful—there are images of women eating their newborn children because of hunger and deprivation. It is all the more compelling to hear a woman's voice crying out in anguish.

Motherhood

I decided that if I weren't married by the time I was forty, I wanted to have a baby on my own. During my thirties there were men who wanted to marry me, but no one I wanted to spend my life with. I didn't want to get married just to have a baby.

Having a baby alone was not a feminist or anti-feminist statement, it was something I clearly wanted to do. Before I became pregnant, I examined a wide range of feelings about having a child alone. I kept having dreams about being pregnant—I was experi-

I don't think I realized I was part of Jewish culture until I went to Israel and then to Russia and started having dreams about my ancestors. It was the first time I believed in the collective unconscious. I tapped into something that is truly ancient.

This year Rebecca experienced the search for the *afikomen* for the first time. Two days later, Rebecca and I went out to buy the first daffodils of spring. She insisted on paying for the daffodils out of her prize money from finding the *afikomen*. I was moved by her generosity and her love.

encing an undeniable inner urge to be a mother. Having Rebecca was the best decision I ever made; it's the greatest thing I have done in my life.

I always wanted Rebecca to be 100 percent Jewish. I'm not religious in the traditional sense, but I did want her father to be Jewish. Judaism is something I feel in my bones, and I wanted Rebecca to have that feeling, too. It is my heritage—it should be hers as well. I have always felt strongly about cultivating my spirit and my inner life. Although we do not partake in Jewish ritual at home, we share in some rituals with my parents.

When I was growing up, my parents—who are Reform Jews—went to temple every Friday night. I went to Sunday school and was confirmed. Later, I went through a period of rebellion, like a lot of people in my generation. I wasn't renouncing my Jewishness or my roots, but I wanted to establish a separate identity. I now accept my parents for who they are and their form of religious expression. I am not observant but Judaism to me still means a devotion to learning, a connection to a European sensibility, and an interest in culture and arts—values I've incorporated in the work I do in my art gallery.

Rebecca has already begun her search for who she is. As she grows and develops, she asserts her own specialness at each stage. Each leap forward is a step toward her own uniqueness; she knows that I believe and trust in her. I am here to help and guide her, but as she grows toward adulthood, she will choose her own path.

NANCY HOFFMAN
New York, New York

Universality

My spirituality has no name. I am all religions and I am no religion. If I limit myself to a particular compartment, that's what I'll get: limitations, isolation, lack of trust, fear. I want to connect with other people without the hindrance of religious boundaries.

I grew up in a town with very few other Jews. My father had a sense of his Jewish heritage, but he thought that being Jewish might impede me. When my mother was asked what religion she was, she said she was French. Although I was voted the most popular girl in ninth grade, the following year I wasn't invited to cotillion balls and country club dances because I was Jewish. I felt a horrible sense of inferiority; I was stigmatized because I was a Jew.

Being Jewish has always been painful for me. It was for this reason that I decided to change the pronunciation of my name—I didn't want people to identify me as Jewish. My family pronounces our name like "Rose-en;" I decided to say it like the rosin of a violin. Rosin has less of a stigma attached to it. Changing the pronunciation of my name felt very good and honest.

Yet I am still unable to shake my childhood feelings of discomfort about being a Jew. I educate people about how we can replace nuclear and space weapons on an international level by developing the space frontier together, and every time I hear about the Israeli participation in the Strategic Defense Initiative and America's Star Wars Research and Development Program, I'm embarrassed by my Jewish heritage. Although I respect and can identify with the Jews protecting their state—their homeland—I also see that they are playing a very old game based on war,

anger, fear, and protectionism. It distresses me to know that the Israelis buy and sell more arms than almost any other country on earth.

In fact, Jews have an opportunity right now to act as leaders for world peace. Jews could say, "We've been outcasts and we've been deprived of human rights for a long time. We want to turn this suffering into positive action and drop out of the arms race." The Israelis could call on the United States and the Soviet Union to sign a verifiable treaty to halt all underground nuclear testing, to ban all weapons from outer space. The Israelis could then help develop a space R&D program that is greater than the magnitude of the weapons industry and that would enhance our security systems through cooperation rather than confrontation.

Some people think that I'm naïve in my hopes. They say that the U.S. Star Wars program can't be stopped because of the economic importance of the military-industrial complex. But the organization I've started, the Institute for Security and Cooperation in Outer Space, has researched countless projects that American industries and the military could work on with the USSR and other countries: communication and education systems, shooting nuclear waste toward the sun, exploring the universe, building space hospitals, farms, hotels, and schools. Cooperative international research and development of the space frontier would help solve the earth's urgent problems of hunger, health, unemployment, and pollution.

The Jews could take on a leadership role in developing these projects by using their well-known business skills. That is a stereotype, but it happens to be true.

They could also use their education, networking, and intelligence information to inform the public about the dangers of space-based weaponry. The Jews could announce that they want to stop the old world game—the game of war—and begin a new one.

The issue of peace in space is a Jewish issue. It is far more crucial than working to get the Jews out of the Soviet Union—a cause that many Jewish organizations spend so much time on. I am sick and tired of hearing that Jews should stick together only to help each other. The earth is at stake!

If Jews took a leadership role in cooperative space development to achieve peace on earth, then I would feel a sense of pride—and hope—as a Jew. But right now, Judaism means nothing more to me than a religion my parents told me I inherited. It is a piece of history. Human beings have since evolved, and we no longer need religions that separate us. We all have bodies made of two-thirds water; our souls are part of the same collective spirit. We need to recognize the oneness of humanity with the universe.

CAROL SUE ROSIN
Washington, D.C.

I have such a prevalent sense that Jewish women—like me—have a strength, a sense of purpose. Although I've denied the Jewish religion for most of my life, when I meet another Jewish woman, I can feel that subtle connection.

Family

I had a complicated birth with my daughter, Rebekah, and lost a second child in miscarriage. Then my husband and I tried fertility procedures but they were very frustrating—we were constantly waiting to take one pill or another. Since we didn't feel a strong need to have biological replications of ourselves, we looked into adoption.

At first, we wanted to adopt a handicapped child since I'm a special education teacher. There were no handicapped children available but there was a healthy biracial baby. We felt we couldn't turn a baby down just because he had a different background, so we adopted Benjamin. A year later, we adopted Joseph. He was a very dark-skinned baby and we knew he'd be difficult to place.

The first time I held Benjamin, I looked at him and thought, "My goodness, he really does have a broad nose." He smelled different from the way Rebekah smelled—probably from the food he was eating—and I thought, I'm not sure I can love a baby like him, a baby who doesn't smell like my own baby. But that feeling only lasted about three minutes.

My aesthetic perceptions have changed since I adopted the boys—I find myself admiring a broad nose or a nice afro—as have my reactions to certain social situations. For example, I was at an election hall where black and white kids were playing; someone scolded only the black kids and told them to quiet down. I felt the frustration that black parents must feel: Their children have to be twice as good as white kids to be considered well-behaved, and twice as bright to be considered intelligent.

But the boys encountered the most difficulties in the Jewish community. One child excluded Joseph from a party, others refused to hold Benjamin's hand during folk dancing, and there were plain nasty comments. I believe that the parents and teachers should have made more of an effort to articulate positive values to the children.

I also feel that what we experienced was not so much racism as a particular parenting attitude among some Jews. These parents seem to be a little afraid of their children. They are unable to impart to them a system of moral values. Instead, the parents imply that a person's feelings are paramount and that there are no true values of right and wrong. This attitude reflects a selfish tendency in American society today.

But my husband and I want to bring up our children with a concern for other people. My daughter and I have been studying passages in the Mishnah, for instance, that deal with responsibility. The underlying concern is: What is our responsibility, as Jews, to other people? Jews are supposed to be an *am kodesh*, a holy people, and that means we have a responsibility to do what is morally right.

We say prayers with our children every day because we want to remember to take nothing for granted: Everything we have is a wonderful gift. That may sound corny, but that is how we raise our children. We feel that Orthodox children too often are taught a lot of rules without learning the concepts behind them, and less observant kids learn that Judaism means how much their parents give to the United Jewish Appeal. We want our children to take their

I was once at a bar mitzvah and overheard a woman behind me say, "Look, there are some *shvartzers* here." I usually don't say anything, but this time I was so angry that I turned around and said, "I don't call Jews here Hebes or Yids and I'd really appreciate it if you didn't call those children *shvartzers*. Besides, those *shvartzers* are my sons!"

lives, as well as their religion, much more seriously. We'd like them to understand that how we act at every moment could either make the world a better place or tear it apart.

This concept of *tikkun olam*, repairing the world, fits in with our general liberal ideals. My husband and I were both influenced by the civil rights movement of the 1960s. We've always felt a tremendous optimism about brotherhood and a belief that everyone is created equal. We may have lost some of our naïveté, but our concerns are still the same. As we've become more traditional Jews, we've been able to place our political and social ideals within the context of Judaism.

We've given our children a faith and a moral structure with which they will be able to solve any future problems they might have. I hope their strong religious background will make it easier for them to deal with life's ups and downs.

We had very good intentions when we adopted our sons, but we couldn't have foreseen all of the long-term implications. Once we took the boys into our family, we made them outsiders, and now I am concerned about what will happen to them when they grow up. I wonder if they will date black non-Jewish women or attempt to date white Jewish women. Having grown up in a white world, will they be able to find a niche in the black world? Or will they always remain on the periphery of different communities—and never quite fit in anywhere?

WENDY DREZEK
San Antonio, Texas

49

Evolution

When I was deciding what I wanted to do with my life, I knew that I wanted to be in a helping profession. The Jewish command to "heal the sick, feed the starving, clothe the naked," always made an impression on me. I'm sure that a lot of people think that veterinary medicine means helping only animals, but the animals don't come into the clinic by themselves. When an animal is sick, it can't call you up and tell you, but clearly the livelihood or happiness of the owner depends upon the animal's health.

I feel complete as a Jew and a vet because I can help people and, at the same time, be intellectually stimulated. Learning as much as I can is part of being Jewish. Many intelligent Christians can question everything in their secular lives, but they have to take a great leap of faith when it comes to their religion. They've been taught that the Bible is literally, fundamentally true; in order to believe certain Christian tenets, people have to disavow science—for me, that's not a learned way to live. But I can question the Bible's version of the story of Creation without feeling that I'm a bad Jew. I think that the world was created through evolution and God was the force behind that process. Science gives me an even greater faith in God; my mind and soul are never in conflict.

Judaism didn't die out along with Greek mythology—it changes, it evolves as we develop a greater understanding of the world and of life. It's adaptable. Orthodox Jews may be right when they say that they've maintained the essence of Judaism, but if Orthodoxy had been the only form of Judaism, we would have lost a hell of a lot of Jews. Judaism survives because of the multitude of differences that exist among Jews. Each of these attitudes safeguards the others and guarantees our survival. Jews have always combined the culture of the country they live in with their own ethnic culture.

The Reform movement in the South made Judaism more accessible to Jews. It also allowed Jews to assimilate and not appear too different from non-Jews. Southern Jews couldn't afford to isolate themselves the way Jews did in the North because they were too dependent on the surrounding Christian community. For example, the Ku Klux Klan used to threaten the Jews, and the Jews became frightened that all non-Jews would stop doing business with them. Jews were aware that if they did anything in protest, they'd stir up anti-Semitic feelings. I've heard Jews say that if it weren't for the blacks, white Christians would focus all of their prejudice against Jews. And this is true. Someone who is prejudiced against one minority harbors those feelings against anyone who is different and unknown.

For that reason, many Reform Jews of my parents' generation didn't want to be involved with anything they considered "too Jewish." About twenty years ago, a recent Jewish immigrant to this country applied for membership at my parents' country club. All of the club members were Reform Jews, and some of them didn't want to let this man in because he seemed so much more Jewish than they were. They felt that all they had done to get accepted by non-Jews would be taken away if very "Jewish" Jews joined the club. It infuriated me to think that Jews would discriminate against members of their own people.

As a Jew, I know what suffering means. At our Passover *seders* we talk about Soviet Jews as well as American blacks. Sometimes, when I'm talking to someone black, I feel like I'm responding with a certain empathy or special concern because I'm Jewish—but Jews don't have a monopoly on compassion.

When I was growing up in Montgomery, Jews seemed to be quite self-conscious about being Jewish. When I was about six years old, for instance, I was getting ready for a party with all of my non-Jewish classmates. My mother told me, "I want you to behave like a nice little girl. Remember, if you're Christian and you're loud, you're just a loud little girl, but if you're Jewish and you're loud, you're a loud little Jew."

I'm not self-conscious about being Jewish in the way my parents' generation was. I want my sons to learn Hebrew so that they can have bar mitzvahs, whereas in my parents' time, this ceremony was considered by some to be too bold a Jewish statement. My kids might go to religious school on Sunday because we live according to the Christian calendar, but at least it's called religious school and not Sunday school. Most Reform Jews my age now want to differentiate what goes on in our temple from what happens in a church.

In a place like Montgomery, there's pressure on Jews to be part of the melting pot, to forget who they are. Montgomery is not a comfortable place to be when you're different and you stick out. Mainstream Americans expect minorities to forsake their cultural and racial differences and be absorbed into the melting pot. To too many people, being American has come to mean being Christian—if not white Anglo-Saxon Protestant.

But if Jews stop practicing and learning about their religion, they're left with nothing. I want my children to know that they don't have to sacrifice their identity in order to be "ideal" Americans. Their being Jewish makes this country a richer place. And they have as much right to be here as anybody else.

LAURIE WEIL MANDELL
Montgomery, Alabama

When I was about eighteen, a Christian friend's mother was killed in a fire. I was very unhappy that she was no longer alive but my friend said, "No, it's wonderful, she's with God now." I asked our rabbi if it was sacrilegious for me to feel sad about someone dying. He told me, "No, Judaism tells us to choose life."

Therapy

I don't find many people who can mirror my Jewish experience. It's hard to explain what it was like being an Arabic Jew who grew up stateless in Japan, or how it feels to listen as a well-meaning Ashkenazic Jew tells non-Jewish friends how Jews traditionally eat apples and honey on Rosh Hashanah. Most American Jews aren't aware that Sephardic Jews from the Middle East and North Africa make a *haroset* of dates and walnuts for Passover!

Since people know little about Arabic Jews, they often ask me why I don't speak Yiddish. I explain that my parents speak Judeo-Arabic, Arabic interspersed with Hebrew words. It excludes Koranic words, unlike the more classical Arabic that Moslems speak.

Yet in spite of some of the cultural differences, Sephardic and Ashkenazic Jews are one people. The Jewish community in which I grew up in Japan was both Sephardi and Ashkenazi, and I saw how we all share the same values, the same ideals, the same passions. My father, for instance, quotes a rabbi from Poland, then a rabbi from Egypt; he laughs at a Yiddish joke; then, when I ask him if he knows any Arabic curses, he laughs and says, "May a donkey bury you!"

My mother's family is thought to have been in Iraq since the Babylonian exile. When she lived in Baghdad, the Jewish quarter had very little contact with the rest of the world. The Jews had a primitive way of life: They were superstitious, poor, oppressed, scared, and trapped without rights. When the Rashid Ali Rebellion occurred in 1939, Jews were randomly killed and raped and their homes looted. My grandmother and her children were saved by a Christian Arab neighbor who told pillagers that my grandmother's was a Christian home. Immediately afterwards, she fled to India, where I was born.

Although we lived in Bombay for four years, my parents were always thinking of some way to get out. There were no business opportunities for my father, and soon he left for Japan. A year later, my mother, brother, and I joined him. It took us a year to leave India because my mother was a stateless refugee. She couldn't even travel under the auspices of Egypt—my father's native country for generations—because she was a Jew. So, using Red Cross papers, we finally were allowed to join my father.

Once in Japan, we applied for visas to come to the United States. My father would have liked to go to Israel, but my mother didn't want to be anywhere near an Arab country. So we waited in Japan, living as stateless Jews for fifteen years, until we could come to America. We made our home in a small suburb outside Kobe. It was 1950, foreigners were a novelty, and the Japanese all stared, giggled, and pointed at us. We were called *gaijin*, which is a pejorative term for foreigner; I was also called *curombo*—the equivalent of "nigger"—because I had much darker skin than the Japanese.

If I had been given three wishes when I was growing up, I would have chosen to be American, blond, and Ashkenazi! If I were blond, the Japanese would have idolized me (now I see that that comes from their own internalized self-hatred). I wanted to be American because I grew up believing that anything West-

I've had so many different cultural and religious influences in my life: an Iraqi-Egyptian heritage, being stateless in India and Japan, going through Catholic and Protestant missionary schools and, finally, coming to America. But there was always one factor, one basic identity that remained clear and constant: I am a Jew.

ern was better than Asian or Oriental—also because in America there were a lot of Jews. They were modern and free. Even though I didn't want to be what I was, I never wanted to stop being a Jew. I had no country, no citizenship; Judaism was the one identity I had. If I wasn't a Jew, what could I have been? That strong sense of my Jewish identity stayed with me when, at eighteen, I arrived in the States to go to college. Once again, I traveled with Red Cross papers.

In college, and later in my own psychotherapy, I grew to understand how the difficulties I experienced in my childhood influenced this "inferiority complex." Yet as I grow, I continue to embrace who I am. I like my brown skin, I like the fact that I grew up in Japan and have such a wide range of experiences, I like being an Arabic Jew.

One of the reasons I became a therapist was because I was working through my own issues of self-esteem and self-acceptance. And the more I resolved my own issues, the better equipped I became to help others. Most people are struggling with a fragile sense of identity for various reasons. I see how some Jews I work with have to come to terms with their own Jewish identity—it is part of who they are. It isn't that we talk about being Jewish all that much, but somehow the issue comes up.

Some of the people I have worked with disavow their Jewishness. They prefer dating non-Jews and say that they are assimilated, cultural Jews only. Often,

once they begin to get in touch with who they are, the issue of being a Jew emerges. When they start feeling better about their mothers and fathers, about their childhoods and their families, they start to feel better about being Jews.

Some of my patients comment on the star of David that I wear, for example. I wore this star all through the Catholic and Christian missionary schools I went to in Japan. Some people say, "The star is so big," or they tell me I'm flaunting something. We explore the meaning of the star and that discussion can evoke a lot of feelings. For me, wearing my *magen David* has a lot to do with wearing my Jewishness in pride: Historically we were forced to do so in shame. Wearing the star is a way to show my Jewish soul. I have a very deep love and connection to our people and our survival. It isn't something I want to hide.

Perhaps Judaism is more than a religion. Jews are an old, old people with a long history. You can be observant, you can be nonobservant, you can study meditation, you can follow Buddhism. It doesn't matter. Once you're a Jew, you're always a Jew. Some kind of Jewish feeling—no matter how buried—is inside you. It is very deep and it has to be recognized. And once you come to terms with being Jewish, you can learn to accept your whole self.

RACHEL WAHBA
San Francisco, California

Image

Many actresses complain that most of the roles available for women are the "hooker" or the "girlfriend" types. Well, you don't see too many hookers or girlfriends named Rivka.

When a Jewish woman surfaces in the plot of a film or television show, she is portrayed as a guilt-ridden, nagging neurotic with egg salad in her teeth. The Jewish woman is rarely the heroine with whom the leading man falls in love. The roles reinforce existing negative stereotypes of Jewish women, which is unfortunate. These stereotyped roles are often written by Jews. I wish these writers would develop positive Jewish role models.

Martha—the dog—was married on "Days of Our Lives" because, as my grandmother would say, "The dog was pregnant and without a husband. . .what a *shande*!"

Contrary to popular belief, the Jewish experience is not necessarily oppressive. My Jewish experiences have always been extremely positive. Religious rituals were never forced on me. Holidays were spent with family and friends whom I love and respect. I guess, though, that I should have seen the influence of the media when my misled, but happy, brothers would bring home *shikse* beauties to our family celebrations. At Passover, I always wanted to ask "The Fifth Question": "How come my brothers don't go for Jewish girls?"

Growing up, I heard an occasional anti-Semitic remark from my non-Jewish and—even worse—my Jewish friends. Still, I've always felt proud of being Jewish. It wasn't until a casting director told me that I was "too Jewish" that I suddenly became aware that I *daven* when I speak. Not wanting to be pigeon-holed as a Jewish character actress, I started taking speech lessons and sitting on my hands. But I quickly realized that my animated delivery is a major part of my success.

That realization is mirrored by the sudden "Jewish resurgence" in Hollywood today. I keep hearing about people in the entertainment industry going "back to be bar-mitzvah." (I probably should, too, since I had stage fright and fainted at my own!)

Despite the Jewish resurgence, a large percentage of industry people have assimilated. They fear that their Jewishness will be misconstrued by others who regard upwardly mobile Jews as greedy rather than successful. Instead, they should question why they're ashamed of who they are. I make a mean brisket and use that to entice my Jewish friends who would otherwise never think to celebrate Passover to come to my *seders*.

The media creates a real dichotomy. On one hand, you see Jewish women in the forefront of social issues. On the other hand, they are perceived as being materialistic and self-centered. As a Jewish woman in the public eye, I feel that I must set some kind of example. So to keep the balance, I strive to be a politically and socially aware person with really great nails.

ARLEEN SORKIN
Los Angeles, California

I almost auditioned for a show because I heard that they were looking for *heymishe* women. It turned out that they wanted Amish women. A minor difference.

Wandering

The Iranian revolution was just beginning when I decided to come to America. I had heard rumors of what might happen in Iran. People said there would be a concentration camp for the Jews. One man told my husband that Jews have always been guests in Iran, but they would not be welcome to live there any more. Despite these danger signs, my family thought I was crazy when I left in 1979. They kept saying nothing terrible was going to happen. But I didn't want to have any regrets. I packed one suitcase and came here, to Los Angeles, with my three sons. I thought I'd stay with my brother for a month and see

I've lost a lot as a Jew. If I weren't a Jew, I wouldn't have had to leave Iran. If my children weren't Jewish, maybe they'd be happier because of all the hatred against us. If they were Moslems or Christians they wouldn't have the same problems. Still, I want them to be good Jews.

America has influenced Iranian Jewish women in a good way. In Iran Jewish girls didn't have bat mitzvahs, but here they do. I want my daughter to learn to read from the Torah and become a bat mitzvah. Women here are starting to have a real Jewish education.

what developed in Iran. My husband stayed in Teheran to finish up with his business. He told me not to worry. If the situation worsened, he'd escape somehow—he'd travel by horse or donkey or even walk to the border.

Things got worse in Iran. Any Jew who did business with Israel or owned large factories was murdered. No trial, nothing; Jews were just taken away. I made the decision to stay in America, and my husband joined us a year and a half later. We left everything behind.

My husband still thinks about going back to Iran, but I say, the past is gone. I want to get American citizenship—it's a way of accepting the fact that Iran is finished for us; it's dead. It's better not to think of ourselves as Iranians any more.

I try to make my children feel safe in America. We celebrate American holidays—I make Thanksgiving dinner—because I want them to be happy, to feel like they belong. But I still don't feel at home here. The way of life is very different for me; even my observance of Judaism has had to change.

In Iran, I was a better Jew. I never cooked or worked on Shabbat. I still won't cook or work, but here I have to drive. What can I do? The temple is far away from my house. My children want to go to services; I can't just sit at home. The first year that I drove to temple on Yom Kippur my heart was killing me.

If we don't continue Jewish traditions, our children won't care about being Jewish. American Jews just want to have fun. In my son's Hebrew school, the kids watch cartoons when they could be learning Torah. The adults eat non-kosher meats; many of them have married non-Jews. They go to exercise class on Saturday. I also exercise—but I would never go jogging on Shabbat.

Jews here have become too American. All they think about is their houses and jobs and how nothing bad can happen to them. But it might. I saw it happen in Iran, in a country I thought Jews could live in forever. Yet when I told a Jewish neighbor that I don't feel secure here, she made fun of me.

I believe that if Jews go to temple and pray, if they do everything according to the Torah, they will be a happy people. Terrible events still occur to people who follow all the laws, but God sometimes wants those things to happen to test people, to see if they'll remain Jewish despite the hardships in their lives. My husband and I were good Jews in Iran but we lost everything we had. I don't get angry, though; I accept the way things are. When I do something wrong, or when I feel guilty about something, I fast for a day and hope that God forgives me.

Nothing has changed for Jews throughout history. When Iranian Jews moved to America, we all thought that we might have to move somewhere else soon. But who knows when or to where? Once again, we're the wandering Jews.

VICTORIA GABAYAN
Los Angeles, California

Tradition

I loved the Jewish environment of my childhood and I want to give my children the same kind of Jewish upbringing. The best way to pass Judaism on is to incorporate it into their environment in a natural way. Since there are four generations of my family living here in Miami, my children are exposed to Judaism not only in our house, where we live with my parents, but in our relatives' homes as well. We all take turns preparing holiday meals and celebrations, so my kids have a strong sense that Judaism is a wonderful, positive part of our entire family's way of life. My closeness to the family comes from my Jewish and Cuban

Three hundred people attended my son's *bris*. The community is so close, and we have so many relatives, that once you start inviting one person, you end up inviting everyone.

background. I immigrated to America when I was three, after Castro came to power. My grandmother had emigrated to Cuba from Kiev. She spoke Yiddish with her children in Cuba and they, in turn, spoke Spanish to their children. Although we've been in the States for many years, we still speak Spanish at home with our children because the language is a part of our family history.

I don't feel that my Cuban, Jewish, and American identities are in conflict. I try to take the best of each and integrate them all into my life. This makes my life rich and interesting and helps me maintain my close connections to the family.

I have a lot of respect for Jewish tradition in particular. My children attend a Jewish day school, as I did, where they learn Jewish subjects, including Hebrew, which is the core of Judaism. They have also learned to pray every morning, which is something I did as a child. I don't feel the need to pray every day the way I used to—with three kids and a full-time job it's also hard to find the time—but that doesn't matter. What is important is that Judaism surrounds my children. They feel it at home, in our relatives' homes, and at school. They see that Judaism means family and tradition; it means following the rhythm of the holidays and the Jewish year. Most importantly, they see that Judaism is a total way of life.

I'm doing for my children what my parents did for me. I'm giving them a basic, emotional connection to Judaism. It's that feeling that will last. How much more can you teach children? I want to educate them, but I don't want to preach.

ELIZABETH MORJAIN
North Miami, Florida

When I was younger, my mother gave me a feeling for Jewish tradition, for the holidays and songs. That's all she needed to do; that's what I want to do with my children. My mother never pointed a gun at my head and said, "You're going to marry a Jew."

Paradise

I came to this country in 1906 when I was fifteen. I'm not ashamed to say that the night before I left Russia my mother showed me how to count to ten. Before then I didn't know one number from the next. About five o'clock the next morning, I traveled by horse and wagon to a ship that brought me to America.

My father worked on one side of a sweatshop, I worked on the other. We made dresses. My heart burned for my father because I saw the way he was sweating and working. I saved a penny and bought two apples: one for him and one for me. He never bought an apple for himself because he was trying to save money for a ticket to send to my mother and sisters.

I worked on a sewing machine fifty-two hours, six days a week. I even worked on Shabbes—something I would never have done in Russia. When I put the thread through the needle that first Shabbes, I thought I was going to die. But nothing happened. I kept working—I knew I had to work so that I could see my mother and sisters again.

The rest of my family finally came to America four years later. Six of us lived in three rooms on the Lower East Side. I slept in the same bed with my Aunt Lena until I was eighteen. Then I got married.

The three *mitzvahs* that married and single women have to do, I always did. I lit candles every Friday night, I went to the *mikvah* every month, and I made *challah*. I don't make *challah* any more because I can't see well enough to put the light on the stove and to measure the honey and oil. Instead, I buy Arnold's kosher *pareve* bread.

I've always kept kosher because I was raised that way. When my mother made a mistake and used the wrong knife for a chicken, she would put the knife in the earth for a day or two, then she would *kasher* it with boiling hot water on the stove. I saw how she lived and I never questioned it. I would never consider living any other way.

But my children don't keep kosher and I won't eat in their homes. A piece of fish, yes, but I'm glad they don't invite me. Who knows what they buy? I don't ask.

So, they come to visit me here, but it's very hard. I can't *kasher* my meat the way I used to. The butcher *kashers* it for me but I don't trust him. I said to God, "I'm blind, you made me blind so I must eat the only meat I can." That's why I'm not going to apologize to God for what I can't do. It's His way and He knows what He's doing.

Maybe God is punishing me. Maybe I did something I shouldn't have done. Maybe I went someplace and ate something that wasn't kosher. Maybe I hurt someone with a word. I was good but I must have sinned. God wouldn't make me suffer like this for nothing. Sometimes I'm in such pain that I feel like I want to die. God should take me already. I don't know what death is like but this is no kind of life.

My husband used to say that I would have a four-legged chair to sit on in Paradise. He said that as a

One night, I heard Einstein speaking on the radio. Someone asked him, "Do you think there's something out there?" Einstein said, "Nobody could have done what God did." If Einstein can believe something is out there, then so can I.

compliment. Whenever someone came to ask for charity, I'd tell my husband, "Give as much as you can." Maybe my husband thought that I'd find a reward in heaven. But I don't know if he believed in it.

I'm not sure if I believe in heaven. I won't say yes and I won't say no because I haven't been there. I don't know if my husband is there, but I do know that I see him in dreams. He lies in bed with me, the way we used to lie together when he was alive. He never says anything, but he moves over next to me.

I am not afraid of dying. I told my sisters not to worry about me when I die because I'll finally be at peace. And I know where I'll be buried, right next to my husband. My grave has been waiting for me for thirty years.

The rabbis don't even know what death is like. All I know is they put my body into the earth. Who knows what will happen to my soul?

FANNY WALD
Brooklyn, New York

Those Jews who become real religious, they're crazy! If a young fellow is in the elevator when I walk in, he turns around and puts his face up close to the wall. He doesn't want to look at me. What can I do to him? I'm an old lady in a housedress!

—*Bessie Meyerowitz*
Brooklyn, New York

68

Second Generation

I am the child of Holocaust survivors. I do not feel I was as traumatized as other children of Holocaust survivors because, for the first few years of my life, I was raised by several caretakers on a kibbutz. Even so, my parents' experience continues to affect my life.

I lived on the kibbutz until I was seven; then my mother took me to America to visit her brother, her only surviving sibling. My mother had received reparation money from the Germans, giving her enough for her passage and mine. Meanwhile, my father and sister stayed on the kibbutz.

Once we arrived, my mother decided to stay longer and find work, thinking she would be able to earn enough money in a short while to send for my father and sister. I am still uncertain why she wanted to leave the kibbutz—she seemed to have been happy there—but she decided that living in America would be best for all of us. Times were hard; she tried to make the right choice. She had no way of knowing that we wouldn't see my father and sister again for more than four years.

My mother is an amazingly strong woman. She worked full time, took care of me, and had a boarder live with us who would babysit in the evening so my mother could attend English classes and then, nursing school. I don't know how she was able to get through it all—I don't think I would be able to do it.

Yet her past experiences haunted her. I remember hearing her cry at night. My mother's parents and sisters were killed in Auschwitz. She managed to stay with one sister throughout the war—they worried about each other so much that they kept each other alive—but that sister died only days after the Americans liberated the camps. Even though the Holocaust changed her life irreparably, my mother told me only two stories about those times. The first is that she was badly beaten by a Jewish policewoman when she was caught stealing potato peels for her sister. The other story was about the time she marched from Auschwitz to Bergen-Belsen. She remembers seeing the sunlight through the leaves of the trees—as if its beauty kept her going. Every time her sister wanted to collapse from fatigue, my mother would tell her, "If you sit down, I'll sit down, and we'll both be shot." Those are the only two stories I know. She told these stories matter-of-factly, without bitterness.

When a friend invited me to attend a meeting for children of Holocaust survivors, I said no. I refuse to think of myself as crippled in some way because of all the terrible things that happened to my parents. But I know their experiences have affected me profoundly. I am filled with dread whenever my mother mentions how someone said something anti-Semitic to her here. I don't think the Germans' attitude toward Jews is unique; there are people all over the world who dislike Jews. I'm convinced that if the economic situation worsens in America, people will use the Jews as scapegoats once again. After all, the Holocaust could happen again anywhere.

That's one of the reasons I want to live in Israel. I don't want my son to grow up in a place where someone might call him a dirty Jew, or where Jews might

I work now in a preschool program, but when I was younger, my dream was to open an orphanage for poor children. I don't know if I felt this way because of my mother's experiences or my own, but I always wanted to help children.

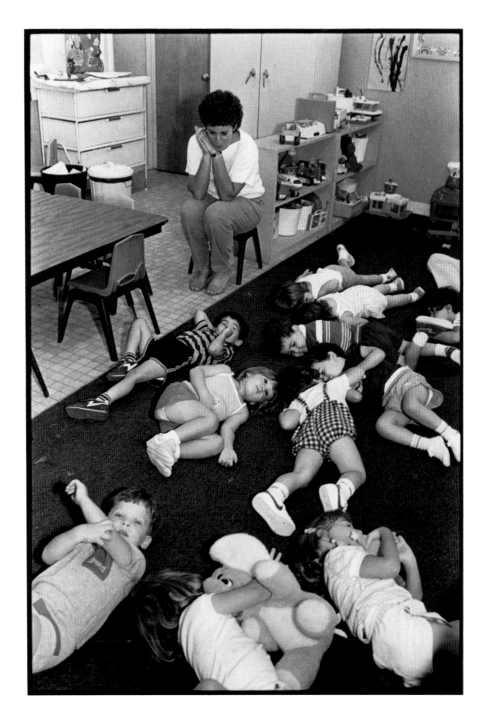

be threatened if the political climate should change. I want to keep my American citizenship, however, because if I ever need an escape route, I could use my passport to get in and out of different countries. But I want to live in Israel. The only way to prevent what happened to my parents from happening to me is by living with other Jews in our own country.

I also feel that in America I have to try much harder to show my son what it means to be a Jew. The longer Jews live here, the less attached they are to being Jewish. My husband and I have started making *kiddush* on Friday night—something we never did before—so that Amir has more of a connection with his Jewish identity. If we were in Israel, he would be aware of Judaism constantly—it would be all around him.

Teaching Amir about being Jewish also means teaching him about the suffering of Jews. My parents' experience makes me feel responsible for explaining the Holocaust to my son. In fact, I want to share this with him a lot more than my parents did with me. My mother tried to shield me from the pain she lived through; I feel that taking care of a child is letting him know what's out there. My mother survived because she saw only beauty around her, denying the horror that was happening. I want my son to be better prepared. It's not a very pretty world.

MICKIE SHUV-AMI
South Kendall, Florida

Hope

I was mistaken for dead a couple of times. Once I was beaten up severely because I was caught stealing potatoes. I was cleaning potatoes for a Sunday dinner for the German soldiers; when you peeled potatoes, you ate as much as you could. I was eating as many raw potatoes as I could when I said to myself: How selfish can I be—my sister has eaten nothing.

So I hid a couple of potatoes for her in my pocket and was caught by a guard. He didn't punish me; but the barrack supervisor, a Jewish woman, saw him question me. She waited for me and beat me up so badly that I lost all sense of pain. My sister stood by watching: She could do nothing to help me. All I could do was block out everything and imagine that I was in a different place. It was a game I used to play when I was a child in the dentist's chair. That's what helped me survive the beating because I was very small and very fragile.

Toward the end of the war, the Germans took us out of Auschwitz and forced us to march away from the border. They were using us for protection—they knew the Allies wouldn't bomb soldiers surrounded by civilians. We were forced to march thirty miles a day; if you sat down, you were shot. Of course, we were given very little to eat. My sister became so tired that she sat down several times. The only way I could force her to get up was to sit down next to her. She got up and began walking again because she didn't want me to be shot along with her. We survived only because we stayed together and helped each other.

Two thousand of us started on the march; twenty-three survived by the time the Americans liberated us at Bergen-Belsen. The big American soldiers were so shocked when they saw us that they cried. I can still remember their faces. They put us in the camp's hospital and gave us all kinds of sweets and crackers and canned meat. As a nurse, I know now that internal bleeding caused by malnutrition worsens when roughage is eaten. But as undernourished as we were, my sister and I were given heavy food to eat. Not knowing that this food would hurt us, my sister and I ate and ate. One morning, I woke up and my sister was dead. She died five days after Liberation. Her name was Esther; that's my daughter Mickie's Hebrew name.

I stayed in the hospital a few more months, and then the Red Cross sent me to Sweden with other female survivors. I had no clothes—I was still wearing my hospital nightgown when I arrived in Sweden. I was a teenager at the time, and a Jewish man and his Swedish wife wanted to adopt me. They told me "We're well-to-do, you'll have a good life." But I didn't want to stay there. I didn't want to be with people who felt sorry for me. I needed to prove that I was still a worthwhile human being. I had suffered so much because I was a Jew that I wanted to go to Israel to build a Jewish country. I felt this was the only way to insure that what happened in Germany would never happen again.

In Israel I helped start a kibbutz with other Hungarian survivors. We began with nothing. We shared our food, our clothes, our money. I stayed there for thirteen years, married, and had two daughters, and then felt I needed a change.

It might be hard to understand why people like my husband and me didn't fight for our lives when we were in the camps. But we had to do what we were told or else we would have been shot. We didn't know that once we went into the showers we wouldn't come out. We didn't know that we were going to die.

When I received some reparation money from the Germans in 1963, I decided to come to America to visit my brother. I wanted to bring my older daughter, Avital, but I didn't want to take her out of school. Instead, I took my younger daughter Mickie. I still feel terribly guilty for leaving Avital behind with my husband, but I thought I would only be gone for a short time.

Because of the war I never finished high school, and it was my dream to complete my education. America afforded me this chance, but I had to work and study in such a way that my daughter's well-being would not be affected. In my middle age, I received my high school diploma; then I went on to nursing school, and eventually received an M.A.

In America, I felt free. I had lived my whole life in a group—in the camps, on the kibbutz—and for the first time, I felt like an individual. I could do what I wanted and build my own kind of life. I thought I would work hard and then send for Avital and my husband. I didn't realize it would take four years.

I tried to give Mickie the best I could under the circumstances. I didn't want to burden her life; I didn't want her to feel guilty because she had all the things I never had as a teenager. Maybe I tried to protect her from hearing about all the terrible experiences that had happened to me. I had many nightmares—about the Holocaust, about Avital—but I didn't want Mickie to hear me crying at night. I don't think I ever told her how my sister died.

After I got out of the camps, I had some very dark moments. I was angry at God for making me suffer too much, I was angry at everything. I hated the Germans, I hated everyone. But through the years I started coming back. I didn't want to forget what had happened, but I had to put things in perspective; I couldn't be bitter forever. I began to believe in God once again. I thought about how Jews are taught to love people and to try to find goodness in them. Not all the Germans were terrible, and I didn't want to instill that kind of hatred in my daughters.

What happened is not what God intended. Even in the camp I tried to be positive. One time we were supposed to go to the gas chambers but there was no room for us. I always imagined that in the next hour something might happen to make things better. Even as a little girl I was taught that we shouldn't give up, that everything is God's will, that tomorrow might bring a change. Judaism is a very positive religion. Jews have suffered throughout history but we've always had some kind of light to hold onto. We are the people of hope.

I appreciate everything in my life; I take nothing for granted. One morning not too long ago, I walked into an elevator smiling. A woman asked me, "How can you smile so early in the morning?" I said, "It's terrible not to be able to get up and enjoy a new morning." Whenever I wake up, I'm happy. I always feel good. A new day is coming.

TOVA BERGER
Brooklyn, New York

My husband doesn't like to dance, but he comes with me and watches while I dance with friends. A few years ago I had an operation to remove cancer in my left leg. The first time I danced after the operation, I cried.

Roots

I was born in Manhattan in 1912. My family was part of a group of solidly German Jewish families who lived on the West Side between 65th Street and 90th Street. It was a group that had drifted very far from religious ritual. I never heard of bar mitzvahs, we never had a *seder* supper. In some ways Judaism was confusing for me—Jewish rituals weren't part of our daily lives—but I never questioned the fact that I was Jewish.

Like other German Jewish families, my family wanted to assimilate, yet we still clung to being Jewish to some extent. I went to Sunday school at Temple Emanuel, but because it didn't seem very important to the family, I skipped a lot of classes. I did learn some Hebrew—but only a little bit. Yet I belonged to a Jewish crowd. All my friends were Jewish, my country club was Jewish, my world was a secular Jewish world.

New York's German Jews all attended the same dances, but you could see a split between the East Side Jews and the West Side Jews. The East Side German Jews were much richer. My husband's grandparents, for example, owned an enormous marble palace on Fifth Avenue while my family lived in an apartment house. We weren't part of what is referred to as "Our Crowd" because we lived on the West Side.

My husband married down, in a sense, because my family wasn't as wealthy as his family—but at least we weren't Russian or Polish! If I had married a Russian or Polish Jew my mother would have disowned me. That would never have occurred, however, because I never had any contact with Russian Jews. There was no mixing between the German Jews and Jews from other countries in the early part of this century.

The German Jews felt superior to the new Russian Jewish immigrants; they were simply prejudiced against them. The German Jews were embarrassed because the Russian Jews seemed poor and uncouth; their language and clothing weren't American, their religious practices were different from those of the German Jews. Yet the German Jews provided a great deal of funding for social agencies that helped the new immigrants get established and Americanized. I always felt the prejudice that the German Jews aimed at the new immigrants was ridiculous and very wrong. Even as a child, I knew that prejudice is not only inconsistent with Jewish concepts but that it was a form of anti-Semitism, and so hurtful to the entire Jewish community.

I think the German Jews felt threatened. They were, in a way, caught between the Jewish and non-Jewish world. The German Jews had encountered little anti-Semitism and they were frightened that the influx of Jews would cause an increase in anti-Jewish feelings.

As World War II approached, anti-Semitism did increase. Many Jews were frightened that what was happening in Germany would also happen here. I remember feeling a sense of insecurity as a Jew during that period. I felt prejudice directed at me.

I'm not happy with the German part of my background. All my family originally came from Germany, and even for me—someone who has such a strong attachment to my roots—I have no desire to trace my family tree back there or even to visit. I don't see how Jews today can accept anything that has to do with the Holocaust.

Some German Jews attempted to end anti-Semitism by pulling in, by denying their Jewishness completely. For example, some of the German Jewish families I knew joined Protestant churches and disappeared into the non-Jewish community. But the prejudice I encountered from non-Jews actually strengthened my feelings of being Jewish. I felt it was important to stand up with confidence and be a Jew. Yet I still wasn't sure what being Jewish meant.

I had to go and find out who I was. I guess I did that by becoming involved in organizations that worked to help other Jews. I've been on the finance board of Temple Emanuel even though I rarely go to services. Every German Jewish family contributed to the Federation of Jewish Philanthropies, and to other Jewish organizations, but no one was more active than I was.

To this day, I still don't know what being Jewish is. Sometimes I think it is a state of mind. Jews are not a race: There are blond Swedish Jews and black African Jews; it isn't just a religion, because Reform, Conservative and Orthodox Jews are all quite different. I think it's mostly a matter of roots. The German part of my background doesn't interest me at all, nor the fact that my family was probably not completely Jewish. There must have been intermarriage or rape—my mother had golden hair and blue eyes—but that's not important to me. I imagine that my family could have been 80 percent non-Jewish, but I only think of the Jewish part.

I have a sense of belonging. I can mingle with an upper-class non-Jewish crowd, but I'm comfortable in the Jewish community. I may not love everybody and they don't all love me but I have a sense of belonging. My grandchildren don't have that feeling—they didn't grow up feeling they were part of a group. I feel fortunate to have had that connection.

Rootlessness is the most devastating thing that can happen to a person. People need to identify with something beyond themselves and their family. I'm friends with all kinds of people, I'm active in all sorts of organizations, but I still feel connected to a Jewish group within the larger American society. That gives me a sense of security. Without that community, I'd feel lost.

ELINOR GUGGENHEIMER
New York, New York

Judaism teaches Jews to be involved in the community. We have to maintain a connection not only to God but also to other people. Many women feel that their Jewishness is best expressed by fulfilling traditional commandments: to bring about peace, to help the strangers in our midst, to perform acts of kindness. By giving of themselves to the community and connecting with others—Jews and non-Jews, women and men—Jewish women participate in the process of *tikkun olam*, repairing the world, a timeless Jewish goal. At the same time, there are some Jewish women who are themselves victims of the world's disrepair. They have been captives of circumstances or strangers in strange lands. Their journey from slavery to freedom gives startling new insights into the modern Jewish experience.

CONNECTIONS

Honor

It's overwhelming to be named Mobilian of the Year. It's probably the most exciting thing that's ever happened to me. In the thirty-nine years that the award has been given, there's never been a woman elected. I'm the first. And I'm the second Jew ever.

I think my award has done more for womanhood in Mobile than anything in a long time. The South really is a male-oriented society, and many women have told me that my winning the award has broken the sex barrier.

But I'm not going to give up the things I like about being a woman because I broke some kind of barrier. There's a thin line between being feminine and being a feminist and it's extremely important to be feminine. One of the reasons I think I was chosen for the award is because I do my work quietly—as a woman, a mother, and a wife—and I enjoy doing it that way. If I were an overbearing, crusading woman, I don't think I would have won the award.

Some feminists think I'm inferior because I stayed at home to raise a family. Professional women look down on me because I don't have a Ph.D., earn money, and work outside the home. But what I do philanthropically and as a volunteer is just as important as what they do.

A lot of Jewish women in the North have the wrong image of southern Jewish women. They assume that because I'm southern, well-dressed, and well-groomed, I must be sitting at home all day drinking coffee and playing bridge. When my husband and I

first attended national meetings for the American-Israeli Public Affairs Committee, for example, women spoke to us as if I weren't there. And one woman said to me, "I'm surprised to hear you speak. I thought you were just a sweet pretty lady." She was amazed that I had something inside my head!

Jewish women down here are not southern belles wearing petticoats and sitting on verandas. I never lived on a plantation or had slaves, nor did anyone in my family. But we southern women do take good care of ourselves physically and we are interested in how we look and what we wear. Maybe the phrase "Jewish American Princess" originated about us. But a true Jewish American Princess cares about nobody except herself, and there are a lot of smart gals down here who have done wonderful things for the community.

Being a Jewish American Princess might be a very good, easy life, but there's a whole world out there. I would have been bored doing nothing all my life. Now, there are times when I get so overinvolved that I want to scream and just play golf, but there are frustrations connected with any work you do—even when you do it for free. I'm blessed because I'm in a good financial position, so I don't need to be paid. I get immense personal satisfaction out of the things I've accomplished with other people. I've seen the fruits of my labor, and that's all the pay I need.

My husband and I are as active in non-Jewish causes as we are in Jewish ones. For my husband's fiftieth birthday, my friends and I donated a lab at Hadassah Hospital in Israel in his honor. For my fiftieth birth-

In my speech at the Mobilian of the Year Award ceremony, I said: "All of my life I have been possessed by a desire to be of service to people. All people must set clearly before themselves their ideas, and then press toward them as a captain steers for his port. Ideals light up the journey of life."

day, he donated another research lab. But we also give to the Jesuit College here in Mobile, and Bishop State, an all-black institution, as well as to numerous local charities. We feel very strongly that our livelihood came from this community and we have an obligation to give to it in return.

I think this attitude of helping all kinds of causes has made the Jewish community in Mobile more accepted and more respected. For example, when people came to tell me I won the Mobilian of the Year Award, they said the ceremony and dinner would be held on a Friday night. I told them I was really sorry, that I didn't want to disrupt things, but that I'm Jewish and even though I don't go to temple every Friday night and do go out sometimes on important occasions, I would feel very uncomfortable being honored publicly on Friday night. I also said that if they couldn't accommodate me, I'd come anyway. The committee made an effort to change the date of the ceremony because they respected my religious beliefs. They were able to postpone the dinner until the next night.

We've never been ashamed of our religion and there's no question that we're Jews. It would have been a lot less troublesome for my children to have gone to school on Jewish holidays, rather than be the only ones who were absent. I would have preferred their having more than three or four Jewish children their age to associate with. But my husband's business is in Mobile and this is where we are going to stay. Instead of feeling negative about being here, we've tried to be positive. But I can't accept Jews who deny their Jewishness in an effort to make their lives easier.

I went to a funeral the other day in the Reform temple's cemetery. The temple is one of the oldest in the country and I was amazed at some of the names on the tombstones. Some of the most prominent non-Jewish—in fact, WASP—families in Mobile have Jewish ancestors. I'd never have known, had I not seen the tombstones—these people want to deny their Jewish ancestry.

Three of my children are married and they all married Jews. That beats the statistics, even in places where there are lots of Jews. I don't think I had any secret ingredient but I've been very lucky and I've prayed a lot. There are a lot worse things that could happen to you in life than being Jewish in Mobile.

ARLENE MITCHELL
Mobile, Alabama

My eldest daughter was the first Jewish girl in Mobile nominated to become a debutante. She declined because of the enormous time commitment—for six months it's one continuous party. You have to be dressed and undressed every five minutes, there are brunches and lunches and dinners and dances. Most Jewish families would rather spend the kind of money that a debutante requires to send their daughter to Europe or to a better college. Our priorities are different.

Diaspora

Twenty-five years ago we moved here to Vermont and started farming. Before that, my husband ran a business in Connecticut, but he always told me how much he wanted to farm. I finally grew tired of hearing him say this, so we started looking for a farm to buy in the Vermont area.

I didn't think being the only Jew in a rural area would be a problem. I've always felt that Jews ghettoize themselves by living so near to one another and that this makes it difficult for their children to grow up and live in a world that is, after all, Christian. But I contend there is anti-Semitism everywhere, whether it's in a small town or a large city. I'll tell you what happened to us.

I don't know how much you've driven along country roads in Vermont, but you're likely to see a loose cow on the road, or even a whole herd, and nobody thinks anything of it. Well, whenever *our* cows were out, the state police came to pay us a visit and told us there were complaints about our cows. We then discovered that someone was sneaking onto our property, cutting our fences, and letting the cows wander out.

A few months after that discovery, our barn burned down. The examiner told us it was the wiring, but we had always taken special care with anything that might cause a fire. It was a very strange experience because the other farmers just stood there, watching our barn burn. Not one of them came to the house and said, "We can help do this, do that." And Vermonters usually help each other. About eight years later, someone confirmed our suspicions—the fire

had indeed been set, and the person who set it had just died. I'm convinced that it was an anti-Semitic act. That's why we moved out of that town to Morrisville. We did want to stay in Vermont, though; we didn't believe everyone in the state was an anti-Semite.

Despite the problems we've had, living on the farm was a very positive experience for us. It made us a close-knit family. After all, when you raise a family on a farm, you can't make plans to go on a picnic on the Fourth of July if your hay happens to be ready for harvesting. We've learned to depend on each other for entertainment, as well as for support in emergency situations. One day, while I was driving the tractor, we saw a storm coming up. As the sky turned black, our five kids knew exactly what to do without being told. To prevent the hay from getting wet in the rain, the kids immediately threw the dry hay into the barn. They saved the entire crop. We knew how to work together—I couldn't ask for anything better than that. Each of our kids has told us that we made the right decision to move here.

As far as their being Jewish, three out of the five are still living as Jews. One daughter in New Hampshire is married to a Jew; another daughter in Arizona is not observant; the third lives nearby and keeps a kosher home. My son who lives here follows our way of life; my other son is married to a Gentile, and I don't think he observes Jewish holidays. I don't intrude on their lives. I don't feel guilty because they have chosen the way they want to live. I always provided a Jewish home for them. It was hard work for me to

My youngest son once designed a SHALOM sign on the roof of a barn he was painting for a neighbor. He had to paint over it, so he recreated SHALOM on our barn. A Jewish teenager who lives near us told me that the SHALOM was "ostentatious, and dared people to knock the chip off your shoulder." But I'll never take it down.

teach them how to live as Jews in a community where there were no other Jews, but it was important for them to learn how to live with their Christian neighbors.

My husband thinks I'm too sensitive about being Jewish. Bernie grew up in a home where Judaism was never stressed. He has been exposed to the religion through me; sometimes I wonder if I put too large a load on his shoulders. It is true that other Jews have moved to Vermont and made it in a social circle. But they might have been so assimilated that they didn't talk about their Jewishness at all. One time, I asked a Jewish couple who had recently moved to the area if they wanted to join the synagogue and the woman told me, "We moved here to get away from all that." I turned to Bernie and said, "So, *nu*, what good is it having a Jew who doesn't want to be too Jewish?"

I never want to hide who I am. The SHALOM on our barn is a political statement. It says, "Here we are. If you don't like Jews, don't come near us. If you don't mind associating with Jews, we're happy to talk with you." Jews see the SHALOM and they come in. Let's face it, there's always something that connects Jews. No matter what their past was, or what they're doing today, Jews feel that connection.

RUTHE SINOW
Morrisville, Vermont

You are looking at the only unsuccessful Jewish business family in the world.

Potential

I knew of only one other Hasidic female butcher when I was working. Since I retired, I haven't heard of any other female kosher butchers. Yet I never thought that being a butcher was unusual—I've always done what I felt I had to do.

The butcher shop was a family operation. I started to work with my husband when I was pregnant with my second child. He was running the store and it was too crowded for him to handle alone. He wasn't strong physically and I was much stronger than he. Thank God I was able to help.

I eventually had eight children—the bigger kids learned quickly to take care of the little ones. My oldest boy did the shopping, the second oldest did the cleaning—I couldn't afford to send any of them to kindergarten. I worked behind the counter and I kept two babies in carriages outside the store. Customers would come in, buy some meat, and sometimes sit with the babies for awhile.

What my husband really wanted to do all his life was study Torah. Whenever we weren't busy in the store, he sat and studied. He has spent his life studying and teaching—he was even offered a job to teach in the suburbs. I told him to turn the job down, though, because I think it's too hard to be a good Jew in the suburbs. Instead, we stayed in Williamsburg. When he retired in 1961, I kept working so that he could study and teach.

The greatest *mitzvah* in life is to learn from holy books. Since men can absorb the teachings of the Torah more than women can, it's wonderful when a woman works so that her husband can learn. The Lord is very good to women. He made the laws lenient for us. Women get as much reward for our work—taking care of our children and supporting our husbands—as men get for learning.

Yet I've always felt a need to do as much as I can as a Jew. When I get up each morning, before I touch anything, I wash my hands and say the blessings. Then I take my orange juice and pill and I *daven*. When I was a young girl, I always tried to sit closer to the men than the women at gatherings. I wanted to hear what the men were saying—they talked about Torah while the women talked nonsense. I wanted to learn. My mother, may she rest in peace, was a smart woman, but she was uneducated—as most women were at the time. My father worried that I wouldn't be able to teach anything to my future children if I knew nothing. He took it upon himself to teach me privately before he went to teach his classes.

Once I had my own sons, I worried about whom they would marry. There were no schools for girls—how would their wives be able to teach their future children if they had not learned enough themselves? I decided to help organize the first girls' yeshiva in Brooklyn, Bais Ya'acov. Now everyone wants their daughters to be educated in Torah.

Yet you know what King Solomon said. That out of a thousand women he couldn't find a righteous one. I've seen all kinds of people and it's true. Women are lightheaded by nature, we're very easy-going, we're not solid enough. If I sit and try to learn Gemara, I can't concentrate. I'm not a master of Hebrew. I can only read simple things.

One night I was working in the store and a man ran in and shouted, "Come quickly!" I ran outside. A woman in the house next door had just given birth. I went outside and cut the umbilical cord with my knife.

There have been only a few very learned women in history—the most famous was Bruria, the wife of Rabbi Meir. She knew as much as her husband did. When he wasn't able to teach his classes, she would go in his place. She is an example of what women can accomplish if we use our potential. Let's hope that once women are educated, their nature will change.

SORAH WEISMAN
Monsey, New York

I always say the prayer for travelers, no matter where I go.

I'm making *lokshn*—noodles—for my granddaughter's wedding.

Tzedaka

Of course, I feel different from the other Supreme Court judges here in North Dakota: I'm a woman *and* I'm a Jew; I also come from a large city, which means I'm an urban person. The other judges here, all Christian and all male, represent the majority of the people in the state.

Even so, being here is paradise for me. Perhaps I'm not altogether realistic because I'm still in a state of euphoria about my appointment as a Supreme Court judge. I hope to contribute to the Court by bringing my intellectual acumen to the study of the law. I'd also like to apply my experience as a woman and as a Jew. Which identity affects me the most? I don't know. How can I even separate them?

Because I'm part of a minority, I'm sensitive to the underdog, the socially disadvantaged, and the powerless. When I was younger, I attributed that sensitivity to my being Jewish. Now that I'm older and more aware of the women's movement, I'd say it's because I'm a woman. I know what it's like to be cut out of the power structure.

There may be people here in North Dakota who might hate me because of my Jewish background, but they represent a ragged, fringe element. The people I am in contact with are decent. I may be the first Jew they've ever met, but they'd be too embarrassed to say so. I don't know how many of my neighbors would have rallied to defend the Jews from Hitler, but then how many of us would risk our lives to save any of our neighbors? Taking such a stand requires heroes, and heroism is an unrealistic standard by which to judge people. Being Jewish has taught me values by which I can help people, not judge them.

The most important value I've learned from my Jewish heritage is the concept of *tzedaka*, which means something more than passive charity. *Tzedaka* is an active concern; it's doing what you can for others, doing even more than you think you can. That might sound simplistic and idealistic, but this concept has taught me that people have intrinsic value. No one should be ignored, patronized, or belittled.

I've tried to pass on the idea of *tzedaka* to my five children. I've also tried to stress to them that Jewishness means the importance of having a strong family and getting a good education. I don't think the trilogy of education, family, and service is as fundamental in Christianity as it is in Judaism. Now that Jews have become integrated into American society, we need to mobilize our resources to integrate these philosophical values. It's wonderful that Jews have achieved equality in American society, but we must hang on to what's good in our Jewish heritage as well. Some Jews who assimilate abandon this, which is a real loss.

Maintaining a Jewish connection keeps us in touch with the best thing about Judaism: its ethics. The ancillary values of religion are what I find positive—whether it's Hillel's "What is hateful to you, do not do to your neighbor," or the Christian interpretation of that doctrine. But we should separate those teachings from the destructive arguments about whose God is better.

As a judge, I try to divorce myself from personal biases—but I can't divorce myself from my experiences. I try to stay aware of my biases so I can take in the facts and then interpret the law. Of course, my experiences have affected me. I'm sensitive to people who have the short end of the bargain.

Holy wars—whether they're waged by ultra-Orthodox Jews or by King Richard's Crusaders—leave me cold. Every religion, including Judaism, fosters prejudice. Jews say all too often, "Our way is the best, Judaism is the truth." It's that kind of superior attitude about our religion that takes us away from the unique principles of Judaism. That's why I'm not a great religion booster. As far as I'm concerned, more wrong than good is done in the name of religion.

BERYL LEVINE
Fargo, North Dakota

If we didn't have religions, I'd have great faith that people could—and would—teach others to be tolerant of one another and do good. But I wouldn't want Judaism to disappear if Christianity and Islam didn't also disappear! I don't think that Jews should lead the way and give up their religion first!

Impact

Banking has traditionally been a male, white, Christian world. The industry promotes a "good old boys" network, which creates an attitude limiting how far women and Jews can rise. Yet the finance industry is changing rapidly. I think that if you do a good job, if you're a team player, you will earn people's respect, succeed, and help break down existing barriers. This attitude has gotten me where I am today—in a powerful senior banking position.

When I started as a bank trainee, there was more prejudice directed toward me as a woman than as a Jew. Later, when I had two master's degrees and was a ranking officer, I was considered a valuable statistic: I helped fill minority quotas. At one bank I was the only Jewish woman among several hundred vice-presidents. Now, there are many more than a dozen Jewish female vice-presidents.

Some of the men I've worked with have resented me. I've had anti-female and anti-Semitic bosses. I even worked for one man who was related to Rudolf Hess. (I wanted to help get him fired but he lost his job himself.) I've run up against prejudiced people and I've tried to change people's minds through a positive attitude. When that approach has failed, I've moved to a more comfortable environment.

A lot of anti-Semitism comes from jealousy—a very dangerous human emotion. Many of my peers resent the loyalty of my clients—both Jewish and non-Jewish—who have followed me with their business when I have changed banks. But I can't let other people's latent prejudice discourage me from doing my best.

That Jews have survived for so long shows not only our will to survive, but our ability. Jews may not be *the* chosen people, but we are *a* chosen people. It's inspiring for me to look at the history of the Jews and see that for such a small percentage of the total world population, we've achieved so much. However, it's sad that often the price we've paid for our achievements is jealousy and hatred.

Jews need to actively create an impact beyond the Jewish community. We can't expect to change other people's negative attitudes toward us by remaining in a closed Jewish environment. Eliminating prejudice can be achieved by working toward solving problems that affect the entire world. One organization I'm involved with helps women in Third World countries become economically self-sufficient. We have to work together. Jews can't change the problems of the world on their own and to think they can is a terrible mistake. Jews need to use their talents to work with other people to build a better world.

On a personal level, the best way for me to combat negative feelings toward Jews is to show my concern for all people—not just Jews. For example, a non-Jewish couple I know asked me to help their son get a job. They don't seem to be anti-Semitic on the surface but who knows, they might have had anti-

Semitic feelings lurking underneath. I feel that when I help someone even in a small way, I help dispel any prejudice that might be there. We must as a group be a caring and understanding people.

Jews should not chase after people—it's a fact of life that not everyone is going to like us. But when we have the opportunity to be in leadership positions, we should work with other people for the betterment of everyone. By acting this way, we help stamp out the ugly face of prejudice.

SUSAN FISHER
New York, New York

My father always asks me what gives me my drive. I don't think a lot about heredity, but that has to have some influence. My grandmother was a driven woman who marched with the suffragettes, and my great-grandfather was a *rebbe*!

Being Jewish isn't something I can talk about, but it's something I know. I think the best thing about the religion is having a bat mitzvah and matzah.
—*Robin Fisher, New York, New York*

96

Leadership

When I first became president of the Council of Jewish Federations I thought, "How did I get to be in this position, speaking for two hundred Federations—approximately five million Jews in the U.S. and Canada? How did I get here?" I was insecure in the beginning, so I consulted three experienced national leaders whom I respected to see if CJF was doing the right thing. Did they realize how much responsibility they were putting in my hands? Did they really think I could do an effective job? The three men I asked (there were no women serving as national leaders other than of women's organizations) looked at me candidly and said, "Yes." That made me feel somewhat more secure.

Still, I was uncertain that I could take the weight of the responsibility. I moved from being president of the local Baltimore Jewish Federation to president of a North American organization. In all my other responsibilities I had moved through the system, going from a chairmanship to a vice-presidency and then to another chairmanship. Here, I made a leap. But I was tested early on—during my first performance as chairman of the CJF's General Assembly. There was a mass demonstration, ostensibly for Ethiopian Jews, but really to give one young man a platform. There could have been an ugly scene, but within the hour I was in the next room with the same man discussing the problems of Ethiopian Jewry. I realized that I had managed to remain calm and composed, I had maintained authority and control of the situation. It was a good test of my abilities.

Since then I have realized that my role is to be more than a conceptualizer and communicator, it is to be a harmonizer as well. I can create a comfortable atmosphere in a meeting so that people can overcome individual differences and agendas and begin to work together on common visions and goals. I know I lead groups well—I've seen how people open up to me. This might be because I'm a woman (although men are also successful organizational leaders), or it could be because I'm the mother of four children—I needed to learn diplomatic skills at the dinner table. I've learned to be a good listener. I may not agree with the ideology of every group that is part of the Jewish community, but each organization and individual has a right to be heard. As a community leader, I don't want to shut anyone out; I prefer being inclusive, not exclusive.

I never consciously planned a leadership career. I feel I am a happy example of circumstance. I was always involved in volunteer organizations from the time I was a child, and gradually I was invited to assume greater responsibilities on higher levels. I was in the right place at the right time, and I think there was a reason for it. I have a sense that a higher authority guides me in my work. There have been too many occasions in my life when I was given opportunities that I never sought out; times when I've given a speech and at the conclusion realized that some of the thoughts didn't occur to me until I was actually speaking. As weird as it may sound, I feel there's something beyond myself involved—my sense of Jewish spirituality.

I have a sense of *bashert*, or destiny: I was given special gifts and talents to help carry out God's covenant with the Jewish people. Tradition teaches that God

It isn't that I have *chutzpah*. Rather, I have the courage to express my convictions and concerns. As a leader, I have to speak out and take a stand. To remain silent would be wrong.

gave us the responsibility of *tikkun olam*—to improve this very imperfect world. I am carrying out my share of the covenant. This is not a burden to me, but it is a serious responsibility. Even as a child, I was concerned about people who were impoverished, homeless, or mistreated. Perhaps it was because my parents spoke about what was happening to Jews in World War II and in Palestine that I understood the hatred and insensitivity that can exist between people. I also knew that I could take on a healing role.

God gave everyone in this world a role to play that includes compassion, caring, and *gemilut hasadim*—acts of loving-kindness. I don't think everyone needs to assume the weight of the world's problems, but if we break the world's problems down to those within our own province, everyone can assume some responsibility to reduce the level of hostility, anger, and pain, and increase the level of understanding. Each of us has the chance to make the world a better place. That is what motivates me, whether I work for the United Way, the March of Dimes, or the Federation of Jewish Philanthropies. I'm not ego-oriented, I don't have aspirations for the next job. I'm only interested in working toward achieving *tikkun olam*.

Currently, I am chairman of the Coalition of North American Jewry on the issue of the "Who is a Jew" Amendment in Israel. I'm also chairman of the National Conference on Soviet Jewry. These are the two most critical issues facing us today. I have met with the Prime Ministers of Israel to discuss the former; I have talked to the President of the United States about the latter. There is no question that I am playing a pivotal role in worldwide Jewish affairs. But, more importantly, I hope I can help shape how the Jewish people deal with crises in the future. I hope we learn to consult with the appropriate parties to hear both sides of an issue, and even a third side, so that decisions are made through dialogue and understanding and not anger.

I'm just one in a long chain of men and women who have helped move the world forward in a positive way. I don't have grandiose ideas about myself; I have no delusions that I am any bigger than a kernel of sand in a time glass. But I do know that I am making a mark.

SHOSHANA CARDIN
Baltimore, Maryland

Before every meeting, I review the various recommendations that people might propose for resolving an issue and try to determine which option will be the best. I don't like to be surprised during a meeting—a good leader needs to be prepared.

Strength

When I was a child, all I ever seemed to hear was, "Let's beat up Hymie, he's a Jew, he's weak." And then a gang of gentile kids would pounce on a Jewish kid and beat him up. What bothered me the most was that the Jewish kids never hit back. They were raised not to fight. This was during and immediately after the Holocaust, when Jews were thought of as meekly walking into the gas chambers. That Jewish kids—as well as European Jews—didn't defend themselves made me think that perhaps Jews really were weak. No one told me this wasn't true.

Yet my mother's attitude toward my own self-defense differed from other Jewish parents. When a non-Jewish girl bullied me, my mother said, "Go out and beat her up." I began to lift weights, and eventually I won a fight against her. It was a small victory and I was still ashamed of being a Jew.

All my friends were Christians. They teased me, saying Jews were funny-looking, rich, and smart. I couldn't relate to that stereotype because I didn't think I was very smart and we certainly weren't rich. I used to take my maiden name, Glickman, and say it was Glickmano so that people would think I was Italian. I became a tough girl who loved to fist fight on the street. I was even head of a gang of Christian kids. Somehow this earned me the respect I needed, but we never picked on weaker kids—I just didn't think that was right.

Then I started studying judo. The sport gave me a feeling of satisfaction and a sense of strength in my mind and spirit as well as my body. Women's judo has now become the most important cause in my life.

Being born a Jew has given me extra drive. If I had felt less oppressed as a child, I might not have become such a good fighter for the inclusion of women's judo in international sports competitions.

Jewish women are not recognized or encouraged in athletics as much as I'd like them to be. The world of sports was closed for Jewish women for a long time, not so much because non-Jews prevented Jewish women from playing, but because of Jewish society's own expectations. When I was younger, and heard people talk about a woman who played basketball, they would say, "She's a good athlete, but of course, she's not Jewish, she's a *shikse.*" Jewish women were encouraged to do serious things—to study religion, to have a family. I try to show young Jewish women that there are other options.

Sports have always been seen by Jews as frivolous, and Jews are not frivolous people. But sports are a serious pursuit. The Maccabiah games give Jews from around the world an opportunity to compete against one another and test their skills. I love the event because I meet Jews from other countries who share the same devotion to sports.

Over the years I've grown prouder to be a Jewish woman; I no longer believe in the myths about Jews being weak. I've seen the strength in myself as well as in other Jews. It is wonderful that Jews have mastered using our minds, but we need to develop our bodies as well.

RUSTY KANOKOGI
Brooklyn, New York

I practice judo with my husband, who is Japanese, and our two children. Our kids will never feel the pain I felt as a child when I was called a weak Jew.

Self-Reliance

It was pure torture for me to be a housewife during the 1950s. I had been one of the best graduate students in my department, and suddenly I was one of the sloppiest housewives on the block. Because of the Freudian hegemony of the 1950s, I felt it was bad enough that I was one educational degree ahead of my husband. Two degrees ahead would surely be castrating—especially since he had flunked out of the master's program. So I stayed home and took care of my son, and I was miserable. I was so lonely for adult interaction that I used to let Bible salesmen come in and talk to me about Jesus just to hear an adult voice.

I felt relieved when I was finally able to return to graduate school in sociology. I was interested in studying women in contemporary society because I felt my gender had prevented me from doing what I had wanted with my life. I decided to do my dissertation on depression in middle-aged women. My mother was depressed at that time and I wanted to explore the reasons for her condition. I felt compelled to research the sociological factors that might explain it. Why were middle-aged women in general prone to depression?

I called my study "Portnoy's Mother's Complaint." Through my research, I discovered that women who were over-involved with and over-protective of their children tended to depression once their children left home. These women had relied on their children for the fulfillment of their emotional needs while their husbands were absorbed in their work. Suddenly the women were left with an empty nest; they felt abandoned and unnecessary. Their lives had no meaning.

I studied five mental hospitals, including one sponsored by a Jewish organization. Another graduate student suggested that I would find many depressed middle-aged women there. I concurred; I thought that Jewish women were more likely to be depressed at this time of their lives due to traditional Jewish, particularly Ashkenazic, family patterns and values. These values emphasized the mother-child bond and the mother's vicarious fulfillment through the accomplishments of her children—particularly her sons. My final analysis proved my theory correct. Jewish women were more inclined to be depressed in middle age compared with other women; Jewish women tended to have had their lives wrapped up in their children, and had no alternative identity—for instance, as a wife or as a worker. They also had high expectations of reciprocity from their children, but they lived in a society where such expectations were not legitimate.

Yet the overprotectiveness of Jewish mothers produced many positive benefits for the children, as sociologist Zena Blau pointed out. She defended Jewish mothers by noting the high achievement of their children and their low infant mortality rate, even when living in slums. However, the pattern tended to be harmful for the mother. By depending on her children for self-worth, she was less likely to develop her own sense of self. The over-involved mother was apt to believe that her children had an obligation to make up for the sacrifices she had made for them.

My study of women and depression has led to other studies about women in society. In my research, I at-

If there is a God up there—or even a Goddess—who's causing so many terrible things to happen in this world, then She shouldn't be prayed to, She should be cursed.

tempt to statistically compare Jewish women to women of other ethnic groups. Although I am not observant, I know I share an identity of fate with Jewish women. The factors influencing their lives are the same factors that influence mine. My research has helped me understand other Jewish women as well as myself.

In my latest study on women and rape avoidance, *Stopping Rape: Successful Survival Strategies* (with Patricia O'Brien), I found that Jewish women are more likely to be raped than to avoid rape when attacked. Another sociologist also found that Jewish women were more likely to be sexually assaulted than women of other ethnicities, except for Native Americans. One reason is that Jewish women are less likely to be brought up knowing how to survive the guerrilla warfare that goes on in our cities. We're less apt to know women who were raped, and less knowledgeable about "street smarts" than, for example, black women. I also found that Jewish women's parents tended to interfere when there were fights with other children; lack of such interference was a factor associated with rape avoidance.

Some Jewish women in the study were conned into going into empty apartments, giving men rides, and other risky behavior because they did not want to seem rude or "paranoid." Jewish women have always been rewarded for being verbally smart, but we were never taught physical self-defense nor specific rape avoidance strategies. Knowledge of self-defense was a factor associated with rape avoidance, and the most effective combination of strategies was yelling and physical resistance. Talking by itself was relatively useless.

Some Jewish women were upset with my rape findings because they thought I was saying that Jewish women are not strong. Others said, "How can you say Jewish women are weak when everyone knows they're so aggressive and assertive." I respond by saying that Jewish women are only verbally aggressive. We're not taught to protect ourselves. Instead, we look to our father, brother, or husband to take care of us.

My work on Jewish women and rape proves that we have to protect ourselves physically, and the backlash leveled against Jewish mothers convinces me that we have to take care of our own emotional needs first. Yet, as Hillel teaches, "If I am only for myself, what am I?" By saying that Jewish women should be more self-reliant, I don't mean to go to the other extreme and say that we must seek independence as an end in itself. We should have the ability and desire to take care of ourselves—and to take care of each other as well.

PAULINE BART
Chicago, Illinois

106

Uncertainty

You have to understand Mobile. The city is isolated geographically from the rest of the country, it's very social, and it's ultra-conservative. A Catholic priest told me that if I had been the Jewish Community Center Director and such a visible Jew fifteen years ago, the Klan would have burned a cross on my lawn.

The Jews here are afraid of exposing themselves. When I tried to organize a Hanukkah torch relay one year, a lot of Jews said, "Jews shouldn't be so public, we need to keep a low profile." I told them that if you don't respect yourself, no one's going to respect you. We finally had the relay, and there was a lot of opposition to it—but only from Jews.

I can't really condemn those people, though, because there's still a lot of anti-Semitism. At the same time, religious fundamentalism is growing. For example, there's a publication here called the *Christian Yellow Pages*. Only stores committed to Jesus can advertise so that good Christians know whom to patronize. When I first saw the Yellow Pages I thought, that's blatant prejudice—it could be the first step toward a coalition against Jews.

Mobile's Jewish organizations agreed with me and it was the first time they took a public stand on any controversial issue. We wrote letters to each advertiser pointing out the nature of the magazine. There will probably be the Christian Yellow Pages for years to come, but at least the Jewish organizations were willing to put themselves on the line.

Jews everywhere want to assimilate, to be like *goyim*, and Mobile's Jews are no exception. Religion takes time and commitment. Christian families here are more personally involved with their church than Jewish families are with their synagogue because Jews don't consider religion a priority. When non-Jewish activities opened up to Jews, the Jewish activities became less important.

I didn't think I'd have a problem living in a small southern town with few Jews because I grew up in Norfolk, Virginia, and spent most of my life in Atlanta. But this is a dying Jewish community. It's the last of the Sunbelt communities—you can't get any further south—and the Jewish community here hasn't grown in a hundred years. What other city in the world can you say that about? When I went to services on Yom Kippur, the temple was empty. I said to the rabbi, "I thought you got more people to come to services," and he said, "Not any more." People haven't moved away, they just don't care.

One local Jewish group, for example, published a cookbook with recipes for Cajun shrimp. I don't observe *kashrut*—I eat shellfish and pork outside my home—but I don't stand for the entire Jewish community. A Jewish institution should represent true Judaism. We have to serve nonkosher meat in the Center because there's nowhere in Mobile to buy kosher meat, but I make sure that we separate meat from dairy. I want to show the children enrolled in the Center's pre-school program that this is what keeping kosher would be like. It's sad to pretend about what might be and not what is, but every *mitzvah* you do is better than nothing at all. I don't think my attitude is hypocritical—I feel I'm being realistic.

If someone asks me at a party, "How come you're eating shrimp?" I say, "That's the nice thing about being Jewish—you can find a comfortable niche for yourself." It might be better if I were completely committed to Jewish observances, but that's not right for me now. I don't feel guilty about this decision, either. You don't have to be a great mathematician to teach math.

I want to help preserve Judaism because it is a good, humane way of life. It teaches a sensitivity to take care of our own as well as other people. I may not believe in Judaism religiously, but philosophically I'm very Jewish. I could be like the Spanish Jews during the Inquisition who didn't follow any Jewish laws. When it came time for them to convert, however, they stood up and said, "I can't accept Jesus because I'm a Jew." Maybe I just have a Jewish soul.

I know that I'm not going to save any Jews here. When I'm at Shabbat services at the Center, I look at the children and know that in fifteen years, none of them will know what Judaism is. And if they do know, it will be a watered-down Judaism. But they sing a Shabbat song to the tune of "When the Saints Come Marching in," and at least that's something they'll remember for the rest of their lives.

Sometimes I feel like I'm on a sinking ship.

MARSHA GREENE
Mobile, Alabama

If my name were Marsha Greenberg, if I looked like the stereotypical Jew—big nose, big *tuches*, overdressed, and loud—I don't think I'd be totally accepted. I don't think I'd be socializing with the Southern good ol' boys.

Congregation

My husband and I joined our synagogue as soon as we moved into our home. It was 1950, shortly after the war, and we felt a need to be with other Jewish people.

We were active in the synagogue from the beginning. The synagogue needed us as much as we needed it. We both came from families that devoted themselves to Judaism, and my mother always volunteered in the Jewish community. At first I was active in the synagogue's sisterhood, then I became a board member, a vice-president, and, eventually, I was the first woman elected as president of the synagogue.

In our congregation we have always tried to raise the level of learning in the community and we're desperate to get young people involved. We have a day-care program for children of working mothers and a summer camp. We're contemplating having full-day programs during holidays so that children can come to synagogue even when their parents can't. We're sensitive to people who need scholarships; we reach out to singles. When we sponsor events, we never charge per couple because we don't want people to think that if they don't have a mate they can't come. We have many adult educational programs and activities to attract more people to the synagogue.

We do everything we can to bring people out, so it's very frustrating when our efforts are unproductive. I don't think there's anything lacking in Judaism, and I don't think it's the synagogue's fault either. People sometimes tell me that the services are boring, that the same things are said over and over. Yet when I ask them how they would like us to change things, they have no ideas. I can appreciate constructive criticism, but it bothers me that people tell me they don't like something and can't tell me what they want instead.

Still, I try to find ways to attract people to our functions. I want to keep the synagogue alive because I feel that if the synagogue goes, Judaism goes. There's something very important about being with your fellow Jews, recognizing a common belief in one God, praying under one roof. People can say prayers at home, but coming to *shul* answers another need. Jews need one another.

Our synagogue is a caring congregation—we're not cold fish. We feel we are a family away from family. With so many children moving away, many older people have turned to us as their *mishpachah*. They need us in times of sorrow and in times of joy. For example, a hundred people came to a party for a man who was celebrating his 99th birthday. And when my husband and I lost one of our sons, the congregation mourned with us.

The synagogue has always been the center of my family's life. That's where I go for knowledge; I've learned from the services, from the people around me. I've become a better person—with higher ethical and moral behavior—because of the synagogue. It's my inspiration—my life.

JEAN LIEDMAN
Philadelphia, Pennsylvania

I'm active in the Women's League for Conservative Judaism, which fights for participation of women in all aspects of Jewish life. Our Sisterhood members can push hard for women's involvement in their own synagogues, but they can't go beyond the rabbi. He has the last say.
(*Jean Liedman, second from right*)

Influence

I often speculate about why women become political because I'm aware of how few women are involved in elective government. I think one reason I went into politics was the Holocaust. Subconsciously, I absorbed the essential knowledge that each of us is responsible for our own life. The only way to safeguard against being a potential victim is to be in a position of active influence and control.

In previous generations, Jews might have known that they needed political power to protect themselves— but they could never act on this awareness. When the Holocaust began, some Jews were led to believe that if they kept quiet, they would not be hurt. I don't blame the victims—the weight of history is too powerful for any individual to oppose—but I do oppose the tendency of people to remain silent in times of trouble, to hope that evil will go away. We have to speak out against injustice at its earliest stages.

I came to the United States in 1940 when I was six years old. My mother was frightened that Hitler would overrun all of Europe and that not even Switzerland, where we were living at the time, would remain neutral and safe. Like other new immigrants, at first I wanted to ignore my background and assimilate, become as invisible as possible. Later, I discovered that my Jewish and European heritage gave me a certain kind of strength. I'm convinced that it isn't enough to simply live our lives within the narrow circumference of our own needs. We're also here on earth to create change for the better in the world around us, and politics is the best vehicle for such change.

I happen to live in a time and country where I can act on my desire to help shape events. Before the women's movement, I might have envisioned a more traditional job for myself, but being a woman—as well as a Jew—is no longer a liability. I'm lucky to live in Vermont, which is a small, hospitable state, and where I've had easier access to the governorship than I might have had elsewhere.

Since I've had these opportunities, I feel it is incumbent upon me to act on my convictions. I believe in a basic moral value system: You have to have a sense of social responsibility. The centuries of struggle that make up Jewish history have also given me the incentive to work for equality and opportunity for other groups and individuals.

There is an amazing number of Jewish women, proportionally, who are involved in politics today. For thousands of years, Jewish women were not encouraged to be intellectual nor to express themselves politically. Instead, they put all their energy into being the so-called Jewish mother. This current burst of energy onto the political scene could be our way of reacting against that narrow vision of a woman's role in life.

MADELEINE KUNIN
Montpelier, Vermont

I feel different from other Vermonters to some extent, but I'm not viewed differently. I'm not a Jewish governor, I'm the governor. The only time I'm referred to as the Jewish governor is when I'm introduced at a Hadassah meeting.

Home

I've always wanted to find a place where I fit in completely, where I truly feel at home—but this dream has yet to be realized.

Although I was raised as a Reform Jew, I began to study Judaism seriously on my own in high school and became more traditionally observant by the time I got to college. Being more or less Orthodox gave me a sense of Jewish identity but, at the same time, it made me feel different from most of the people I grew up with, Jewish as well as gentile.

Walking around my San Antonio neighborhood, I felt alienated. I would think, "What am I doing living in such a *goyish* neighborhood?" I thought that when I moved to Israel I would automatically feel like I belonged. To my dismay, however, when I was riding on a bus in Tel Aviv a few months later, I found myself thinking, "I really don't fit in here, either." I had discovered that in America I defined myself as a Jew, and in Israel I was an American.

I went to Israel at age nineteen, full of ideals and illusions. I expected to find my Paradise Lost, my heavenly Jerusalem—the place where I'd feel completely at home—but my expectations were very unrealistic. I was determined to transform myself into a *sabra*, a native-born Israeli. I changed my name, I worked hard to speak with an Israeli accent. People still considered me an American, however, and it wasn't until I heard a recording of Golda Meir speaking Hebrew with a strong American accent that I decided, if it's good enough for her, it's good enough for me.

I stayed in Israel for four years. I married an Israeli, had my first two daughters, and began to integrate my identity as an American and an Israeli. But there were plenty of times when I missed America. One major problem was a loss of self-esteem. In San Antonio, people knew me, knew my family; in Israel I tended to feel like a *nebbish*. I had to rebuild my identity. Culture shock was another problem. For example, I've mostly found Texans to be polite and easy-going—compared to them, Israelis were blunt and rude. Israelis whom I didn't know felt free to be critical of me, or argue with me in the supermarket checkout line. Yet with equal disregard for ceremony, Israelis could also be hospitable, warm, and helpful. It's true that Israel seems like one big family—but that also means putting up with a lot of family fights.

Despite all the difficulties, I felt a sense of elation just being in Israel. I felt needed, as though my very presence played a part in Jewish history. One day, for instance, my husband and I climbed Mount Zion. Before the Six Day War, he told me, that vantage point was the closest that Jews could get to the Western Wall. I looked around at the Jerusalem stones, the spring blossoms, the Mediterranean sky, and thought of my ancestors celebrating Passover in dark *shtetls* in Poland, and how each year they'd say, "Next year in Jerusalem." And there I was, fulfilling not only my personal dream and my family's dream, but the dream of the entire Jewish people.

Nevertheless, a variety of circumstances brought me back to Texas. My father had been killed in an accident, and I wanted to return to San Antonio to be closer to my mother. I missed my family a lot. My husband also thought it would be a good opportunity for him to finish college in the United States without

There are many cultural differences between my husband and me. He spent ten years in an Israeli transit camp; I grew up a privileged daughter of an American doctor. I'm Ashkenazi; he's Sephardi. If we move to Israel, I'd like to work with an organization that forges ties between diverse groups of Jews. My work ahead is to bridge gaps.

army reserve duty and some of the other pressures of Israeli life.

Now that I've returned to this city, I lead a basically happy life. I have friends and I'm very involved with the Jewish community. But I'm still aware that I'm not entirely at home here. The years of learning about my heritage and of living in Israel transformed my way of thinking. I might be driving to a store—something other San Antonians do—but unlike most of them, I'm often thinking about Jewish ideas. If I have a problem, I try to use Jewish sources to solve it. When I do something kind, I don't think I'm being "a nice person"; I see it as a *mitzvah*. Wherever I am, I see the world through Jewish eyes.

I feel both American and Israeli, although I am uncomfortable saying that because Jews in the Diaspora have always been accused of dual loyalties. I am a Jewish American culturally, intellectually, and linguistically, but I get choked up when I hear "Hatikvah," the Israeli national anthem, and not when I hear "The Star-Spangled Banner." America is my native country; Israel is my spiritual homeland. My soul pulls me back to Israel, yet I'm not sure when I can make the commitment to live there again. I'm torn between both places, and I sometimes wonder if, wherever I choose to live, I'll ever feel completely at home.

JULIE HILTON DANAN
San Antonio, Texas

The *pintele Yid* means that there is a drop of Jewishness in all Jews, no matter how assimilated they might be. I know I also have a *pintele* Texan—a part of me is really Texan. I'm very happy that my daughters are spending part of their childhood in the house I grew up in and in my hometown so that they understand where I come from. I don't want to feel like a stranger to them.

Support

When I married my husband, I was aware that we had a lot of problems, but I thought that love would conquer all. I tried anything that I could to stay married. But when I was seven months pregnant with my second child—my oldest was only a year old—my marriage finally fell apart.

I gave birth to my second son, Luke, in Chicago where my parents live. Then I moved back to Seattle, where I had lived for a while with my husband. I thought the city offered more support for families than Chicago, not to mention better weather. I tried to get my husband to visit me so that he could see the baby, but he refused. A few weeks later he was gone.

I had no money and I couldn't pay the rent, so I went on welfare to receive emergency assistance. One of my ex-friends said to me, "I would never go on welfare. I'd go live with my parents." But I couldn't do that. My situation isn't my parents' responsibility, it's my ex-husband's. Right now they help me out as much as they can: They send me care packages, and they give me whatever help they legally can within the welfare system. I have thought about getting a full-time job, but I would go into debt just to pay for child care costs. And returning to law school—something I dream about—is also out of the question right now. I have to wait until my kids are in school before I can realistically plan full-time work or full-time schooling. Besides, it's extremely important to me that I raise my children myself, especially through their first five years. I don't want them in full-time day care.

I grew up in a Jewish home where my parents stressed a pursuit of excellence, an interest in culture (theater, ballet, classical music), and a philosophy of investigating, thinking about ideas. I want the same thing for my children—music lessons, for instance—and it really distresses me to think that I might not be able to provide all that for them. I encourage them with love; I try to instill in them a desire for intellectual investigation. I want them to have the inner resources they need to counterbalance the disadvantages they already face.

I've always felt that one area in which Jewish attitudes are superior to other people's is that we have a greater sense of tolerance and concern for others. We aren't as dogmatic nor as judgmental, and I still think this is true. The Jewish community runs a food bank and counseling services to help people in need. When I explained my situation to the local temple, I was invited to join without paying a membership fee. Some people have been sensitive to my financial problems. They haven't, however, reached out to give me the friendship and emotional support I need.

I am involved in organizing low-income and welfare women working toward welfare reforms and other women's concerns. But that isn't really a community of people that I can belong to. I want to be part of the Jewish community because it is something for my kids and me to hold onto together.

I tried to reach out to Jewish mothers in one temple here. I thought it would be nice to have a group of

I've always been a feminist but I've become more militant. I'm angry at the way most men refuse to pay child support or even acknowledge the growing ranks of women and children living in poverty. But my subconscious is still in the 1950s. I'm still waiting for a man to save me and take me away from all this. I'm still waiting for my knight in shining armor.

women meet to talk about parenting concerns as well as women's issues. A few women told me that their kids drive them crazy, they have to have help, and they can't imagine raising kids by themselves. They tell me how brave and courageous I am. But that never translated into support or friendship or even inviting my kids over to play with theirs. They showed no empathy for my situation—but what happened to me could just as easily happen to them. Their husbands could walk out on them: Divorce is common these days, not every marriage lasts forever. I'm troubled that Jewish women, especially those in the upper middle class, don't prepare themselves for the possibility of divorce or poverty.

It would be nice if the Jewish community could pull together to become more of a family. Ideally, we could all stretch a little bit—invite other people into our lives—because we don't have large, extended families any more. Older people could become foster grandparents and people like me could be foster grandchildren. Temples and Jewish community centers could do more outreach programs for people who are new and newly single in the area. They could help organize clubs for single parents that don't cost money to join. It's wonderful that Jews help out charitably, but communal support is more important. I would like to see more Jews making a commitment to help one another.

I believe that I share a heritage with other Jews— that's what makes me feel part of a people. But underlying that is a belief in God, without which Judaism wouldn't mean as much. There is something beyond us. God is in charge of the order and reason in the world.

Sometimes I get very angry and bitter about my situation. The pressure of raising two children on my own is enormous, and I am under the most stress I've ever had to endure. If I had to depend solely on myself, I would expect perfection—I wouldn't be able to accept myself and my own shortcomings. But feeling that God supports me and drives my life reminds me that, like other human beings, I can be fallible. Only God is infallible. Understanding this is the only way for me to forgive myself for the mistakes I've made in my life.

MELANIE GRONER
Seattle, Washington

I really would like to create a Jewish home. I'd like to have Jewish books, Israeli posters, and special Jewish paraphernalia—but those things are not yet in the budget. Right now, I consider it a great accomplishment if I can feed my children three nutritional meals a day and get them to say the *Shema* prayer at bedtime.

Allegiances

Being Jewish is a dual citizenship. I'm an American and I'm a Jew: Both identities are equally important to me. As a Jew, I'm part of a family that begins with my own family and then extends out in concentric circles to include the Jews in the community, in America, and in the world. There's a link, an understanding among all Jews, that we've come through the ages and have survived all of these years. Being part of this extended Jewish family gives me a certain feeling that is more important than the Jewish religious practices that I may or may not choose to follow.

We belong to a Reform temple. My husband initially wanted to join a Conservative temple—we were both brought up in families who belonged to Conservative temples—but when I asked him if he were willing to attend as often as the Conservative temple suggested, he changed his mind. If you aren't following the observances of a Conservative temple, then don't belong to one. You shouldn't be hypocritical.

I don't feel guilty for being less observant than other Jews. Some might say we're shortcutting religion, but I've always believed that Jews have the right to observe and celebrate in whatever fashion they prefer. When my family has to choose between going to a baseball game, out to dinner, or to temple, going to temple does not win out. I don't feel the need to do what's expected of me as a Jew—only what I want to do.

I don't mean to sound as though I'm making excuses, but Jewish life no longer revolves around the temple the way it did in earlier times. Jews all over the world practice their religion in different ways today. You make your choices.

We chose to move into a predominantly Jewish community, however, so that our sons could associate with other Jewish children and learn to be proud of their Jewishness. I always intended for them to be educated in the formal Jewish tradition and to be bar-mitzvahed, and they were. I can state right now that I'd like them to marry girls—ladies—of the Jewish faith. I've told them that living in a Jewish family means sharing special times, and if they don't marry Jewish girls, they might have to give up those times.

My family's Jewish life consists of daily occurrences that might spark a whole discussion about Judaism. The other day, for example, my oldest son was making a ham and bagel sandwich. Even though we're not kosher, the sandwich looked like a strange combination to me. We talked about why Jews have traditionally not eaten ham, and I told him why I don't think eating ham is sacrilegious today. I think the tradition started for health reasons: Food was *kashered* to make it safer to eat, and pork was known to be less sanitary. Reform Judaism has changed rules like that—restrictive rules—so that Jews can conform to modern-day living.

We Jews aren't above learning and incorporating other practices into our lives. People grow by welcoming new ideas and by coming into contact with other societies. When my grandmother came to

One of my sons injured his knee, so I took him to a doctor. The doctor was vague in explaining what was wrong. When I asked him to be specific, he said, "Oh, you're a Jewish mother, you have to know everything." I said, "I'm a mother and I'm concerned. What does being Jewish have to do with it?" If that doctor, who is Jewish, considers me a typical Jewish mother, that's his problem. I have to accept how some people choose to judge me.

122

America, for instance, she wanted to learn English so that she could assimilate and become American. The Cubans here in Miami refuse to speak English and to adapt to their new culture. Frankly, I think their attitude conflicts with the American way of life.

Some might argue that as Jews become more Americanized, Jewish culture will become so watered down that in four or five generations there won't be anything left. Although we may have already lost some parts of our Yiddish culture and traditions, I don't think the process has been detrimental to us. Jews have to go beyond the ghetto. I'd like to keep some of our traditions alive but I want to incorporate them into my modern, so to speak American, way of life.

I feel American. But I remember reading that the German Jews felt that they were Germans first and that nothing bad could ever happen to them as Germans. A part of what I love about America is the freedom we have—I don't think the Holocaust would be allowed to happen here. But another part of me feels you can't be too sure of the future. You can never rule anything out.

LYNN HUBERMAN
Miami, Florida

Purpose

Deafness is invisible. A blind person's disability is obvious, and so is the disability of someone in a wheelchair, but deafness is completely unseen to most people. Deafness is not invisible to me, however. I can recognize another deaf person on a bus just by the way that person uses his or her eyes. Deaf people know other deaf people the way Jews know other Jews.

My parents don't know how I became deaf. My mother says she noticed nothing unusual when I was born. I looked normal, I sounded normal, but I didn't seem to respond to sounds around me. When I was two, a deaf neighbor told my parents that he thought I was deaf. My parents took me to a doctor who informed them that I was deaf and would never learn to talk.

My parents were really upset. They got me hearing aids and sent me to speech classes. I was in a self-contained classroom for speech-impaired and hard-of-hearing children at a public elementary school until I was in sixth grade. Then I went to a hearing public school in my hometown. At the time, there was no other appropriate school setting for me, and my parents didn't want to send me to a residential school for the deaf. My parents wanted me to fit as normally as possible into the hearing world.

Yet no matter how hard I tried, I couldn't fit into the hearing world. I knew something made me different from everyone else, but I wasn't sure what. People my age were a little afraid of me, and I felt very lonely. I had no deaf community, yet I didn't fully fit into the hearing world. It was not until I went to college at the Rochester Institute of Technology's National Technical Institute for the Deaf that I made good, lasting deaf friends and met other deaf Jewish people who told me they had experienced the same kind of pressure to overcome their disabilities and to achieve. It became clear to me that Jews place a high value on success—no matter what obstacles might exist.

My parents asked if I would speak at my brother's bar mitzvah when I was sixteen. I was frightened I would make a fool of myself. After I read aloud a passage from the Torah, my mother told me that some people cried because they didn't realize I spoke so well for a deaf person, yet I felt shy and embarrassed. Looking back, I would have felt more comfortable using sign language and an interpreter, but at the time, neither my family nor I was aware of that option. When I was older, I finally understood what adjusting to my deafness meant. It means doing what feels most comfortable for me—even if that makes me seem different in some ways from the hearing community.

Now that I'm more confident of what it means to me to be deaf, I feel it's my responsibility to help educate the Jewish community about other deaf Jews. I want synagogues and Jewish groups to reach out more effectively to the deaf community. They can hire sign-language interpreters at services, sponsor Jewish deaf storytellers, and make events more accessible to deaf Jews, as well as to people with other disabilities. The Jewish community, like the rest of society, is slowly awakening to the needs of all kinds of people.

When I visited Israel a few years ago, I realized how little I understood about Judaism and the history of the Jewish people. (I had gone to our temple's religious school, but since I didn't understand what was going on, I stopped going when I was about fifteen.) During the last part of my trip, I told my mother that I thought I had missed so much and she told me, "Perhaps you missed a lot of information about Judaism and other things, but so did I!" I'm learning more about being Jewish now, through some close friends and my involvement with a group for deaf Jewish youth.

Hearing people may think that being deaf is lonely and isolating: I might not be able to understand music or voices, but I feel that God gave me my deafness for a reason. I am part of a small, special minority, and I can teach people about what being deaf means. In some ways, being deaf is a blessing—it gives me a purpose in this world.

JOY HOLTZMAN
Boston, Massachusetts

I need to be an advocate a good amount of the time for the deaf people I work with. I also need to advocate for my own personal rights—something as simple as requesting that a sign language interpreter be present at a "hearing function," for example. I also need and want time to just relax, to take a break from advocating for the deaf community and enjoy myself as a person.

Mitzvah

I joined the National Council of Jewish Women New York Section in 1973. My eldest son was mortally ill and I needed something to do to take my mind off his situation. At first I volunteered in the children's library program. Later I became involved in fundraising events. In 1983, I was asked to be co-chairwoman of a soup kitchen that the NCJW New York Section wanted to start up.

My work in the soup kitchen is the most satisfying thing I've ever done. I know I'm doing the best I can to ease the problem of hunger in New York. In addition to serving a hot meal to 105 people a week, we give fifty take-out lunch bags to those we can't seat. Compared to the enormity of the hunger problem, our work might seem like a pebble on the beach. But put a lot of soup kitchens together and they add up.

About 15 percent of the soup kitchen's clients are Jews. Some of them are elderly women who live at borderline poverty. They are emotionally hungry. When they see me, they always say, "Hello, how are you darling?" It's meaningful for them to come and eat with people.

There are discomforts and sadnesses to the work. Some women have tried to volunteer, but they've felt too sad seeing the people—they couldn't come back. Others stay in the kitchen and only dish out the food. It is not always the most pleasant place to be. Some of the clients are malodorous, for example. But I have to deal with it. I've had tragedies in my life and I'm tough. I can handle queasiness. I can work in the soup kitchen and feel badly for the people; then I can go home and forget about them for a while. I'm never burned out, I just go on with my life.

I'm not a Lady Bountiful. I don't go to the soup kitchen with white gloves on. I put on comfortable clothes and sneakers and go there to really work. I'm just a person helping other people. I'm doing a *mitzvah*. It's a Jewish concept to help others, to give unto them. Anyone who has money can write a check. But I think you get more satisfaction working with the people directly.

People always ask, "What do you do?" in social situations. I'm glad I can say I'm a volunteer in a nonprofit organization and I help run a soup kitchen. This is my job and I have a great sense of responsibility about what I do. I would seem very flip if all I could say was that I get my nails done, play a lot of tennis, and go to fancy restaurants. I don't necessarily feel guilty about all that I have, but I do feel very lucky. Since I don't have to work to earn money, I'd be selfish if I didn't do something for others. Women help one another when we work together. A woman alone wouldn't be able to do much, but she serves a purpose when she's a link in a chain of strength. The chain links Jews to one another, to tradition, to helping Jews and other people. And I'm proud to be part of that chain.

BERNICE FRIEDES
New York, New York

Some volunteers say they can sympathize with the people who come to the soup kitchen because they feel, "There but for the grace of God go I." I don't feel that way—I can't envision myself being in their position unless this country falls apart. Yet I feel for them, not because I can see myself where they are, but because they're human beings and they're suffering. It's terrible to see people in pain. (*Bernice Friedes, on left*)

Matchmaker

I'll tell you a true story. There were two sisters who were all alone in the world. They had no parents, no family, no one but each other. The older sister came to see me first. She was not very attractive or educated, which gave me very little to work with. But she was fortunate because there was a man who had just joined my matchmaking service. He had recently been divorced and he was very depressed—he wanted me to find someone to focus on him and adore him. She fit the bill and he married her. Then the other sister came in—now she had no one left in the world. We got her married, too. What else in life can give you such a wonderful feeling when you help two lonely girls get married? I enabled them to start their own homes and families.

My service, The Matchmakers, has been in business since 1981. My partner, Judy Friedman, and I have made over 120 marriages. I'm very proud of that. I feel that I am doing something to help Jewish men and women meet one another and marry. I'm not doing this for the money. I'm a matchmaker because I am concerned about the rate of intermarriage. Jewish people erase themselves through intermarriage; it weakens the links between generations. Even if the non-Jewish partner converts, that partner can't contribute the tradition, the genes, and the family that is a result of a marriage between two Jewish people.

I decided to start a dating service because I saw that Jewish people had no place to meet one another in a respectable way. At first I organized cultural events in a Jewish social hall. But the programs weren't working—girls sat on one side of the room, guys on the other. That's when I realized that I needed to match people up on a one-to-one basis.

It's still a very difficult job. Even today, with all our experience, my partner and I work on a hit-and-miss basis. Sometimes we think two people are a perfect match and they don't like each other at all. Other times, Judy will match people up and I'll ask, "How did you have the nerve to do that?" and it will work out. As much as we think we know what makes two people love each other, we really don't. There is an x factor—chemistry.

Unlike other matchmaking services, Judy and I often work behind the scenes. We matched up two people, for example, whom we thought would be a perfect pair. But he said that she didn't want to date, and she said that he was too arrogant. We told him that she *did* want to date, and we told her that he wasn't really haughty. They went out one more time—only to please us—and now they are getting married. I combine my expertise with a little "Jewish mothering." I've told some girls the way they dress could be more flattering; I've told some of the men that they should go to aerobics class. I am concerned about them and want to help them find their partner for life.

Some women think that because I'm a matchmaker, I have a stockroom in the back filled with great men and they can specify what they want. They tell me: He must be tall, and have dark, curly hair, he must be a financial wizard and he must have a sense of humor. I think that if you can just get a guy to care for you, support you, and be your friend, you have a lot.

Going to a matchmaker seemed like an old-fashioned thing to do, but I was tired of being single and I wanted to meet someone outside the circle of people I knew. There's no doubt in my mind that if I hadn't gone to a matchmaker, I wouldn't be as happy as I am now.

—*Pam Smith*
Chicago, Illinois

Jewish men and women have a lot of expectations, as well as stereotypes, about one another. The women think the men are *nebbishes,* the men say the women are spoiled. Yet most Jewish girls are hard-working and willing to do their share to help out in the house. Of course, there are a few girls whose generous fathers have spoiled them, but they are, thankfully, a tiny minority. Many men are shy at first, but with a little encouragement they gain self-assurance.

Another type of Jewish women I see must have received the opposite message from their parents. They were told to go out and accomplish something, to be professionals. These women have two degrees, they've built up careers, and then they wake up one day and ask, "Where am I?" They don't have a home or a family or a husband, and they panic. A 39-year-old doctor asked me to find a man for her. She is at the top of her field, she makes a lot of money. Where am I going to get a guy to match up with her? The great guys her age have all been taken. But I still try to be optimistic—you only need to find *one* man!

If I had a daughter who was willing to listen to me, I would tell her: Find a loving partner, establish a family, and then pursue a career. I don't think supermoms are happier—they work all day, then they run home to do everything for everybody. Men might appreciate a talented and driven woman, but don't they also really want a woman who's less harried and more nurturing?

In my mother's day, in Europe, the only way that marriages ever took place was when a *shadchen,* a matchmaker, arranged them. He or she went to a house and looked it over, met the parents and ascertained how observant they were, checked out their son and then found a girl for him. My father, for example, came from a wealthy family. He told the

shadchen, "Find me a girl, and if she is really nice, I won't ask for a dowry." The *shadchen* thought of my mother, whose mother was recently widowed with a large family. He said to my grandmother, "I've found the best man for your daughter. He's not asking for a dowry, his father has a mill where they grind the wheat, so she will always have something to eat." That is how my parents' marriage was arranged. This successful relationship lasted over sixty years.

When I was of marriageable age, though, my parents didn't call on a *shadchen.* They were "modernized" and expected me to find my own true love. I went to dances, lectures, singles events; I went out on a lot of blind dates; and eventually met my husband at a Jewish function. Perhaps being a matchmaker is one way for me to spare someone else this trouble.

If a woman comes to my service who really wants to be married, she will most likely get married. But she has to be willing to settle for Mr. Alright instead of Mr. Right. A successful lawyer, for example, married a guy who worked in a drugstore in a poor neighborhood. Other women might not have been as flexible as she was, but she recognized that he had integrity and intelligence and he loved her. They are one of the happiest couples we have helped.

With all the single people around, I don't know if I still believe in the Jewish concept of *bashert*—that there is someone fated for each person. There are so many singles who need my help—can I find their *bashert?* But I do believe that if you are fortunate enough to find your true love and build a life together, then you are very lucky. That is about as happy as you can be in this world.

IRENE NATHAN
Chicago, Illinois

Divorce

Jews lost a lot when they moved away from one another and assimilated into the American society at large. In addition to dropping our Yiddish language, we gave up some of our power to control our religious affairs. I felt this in a strong, personal way a few years ago, when my husband and I divorced. For four years, he refused to give me a *get*, a divorce document. Without a *get*, I was unable to remarry or even date because I was considered an *agunah*—a woman anchored to an unwanted marriage.

When you're married, you're supposed to cover your hair out of modesty. Once I received my *get*, I thought I might take off my *sheytl*, but a rabbi told me that I should keep it on.

My husband told me he would present me with a *get* only when I agreed to joint custody of our four children, something I was unwilling to do. They were under six at the time, and I thought it would be psychologically damaging for them to be moved from my house to his every week. He disagreed, and there was nothing I could do but sit and wait. He hired a lawyer, I hired a lawyer, and we negotiated back and forth. I felt totally helpless. If I had chosen to remarry in a civil ceremony, I would have been considered an adulteress and any children I might have had would be seen as *mamzerim*, bastards, under Jewish law.

Unfortunately, my husband's behavior is not uncommon. Some men blackmail their wives and withhold

Practically speaking, it's much easier for me to wear a wig—I can be ready to go out in fifteen minutes.

I've also turned the discipline of wearing a *sheytl* into something positive. I can be a redhead one minute, then have long blond tresses, and then choose a Jean Harlow look. I have the chance to live out every woman's fantasy.

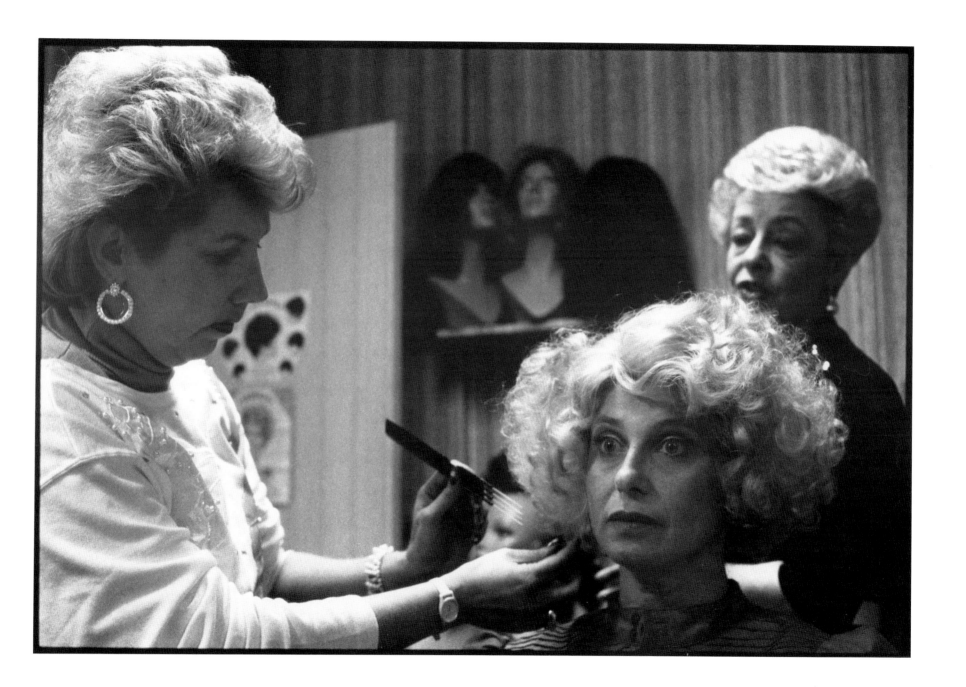

the *get* until they are paid hundreds of thousands of dollars. Others decline to give a woman a *get* to punish her for imagined or real wrongs. The four years that I had to wait are a drop in the bucket when compared to a woman who's waited for ten years! In fact, a woman can be trapped as an *agunah* forever if she has no way to ransom her freedom.

People say, "Judaism is unfair because only the man can give the *get* to his wife, and he doesn't need a *get* from her." This may be true, but Jewish law also permits you to beat him within an inch of his life until he says, "Yes, I will give you the *get*." So, the problem is not with Jewish law. The problem is that Jewish women have fallen through the cracks between *halakhah*—Jewish law—and American secular law. American law doesn't interfere with the first part of Jewish law concerning divorce—that a Jewish man has to give a *get*—but it does interfere with the second part, that you can beat him up if he doesn't give it to you. A woman who hires people to beat up her ex-husband might wind up in jail.

I don't think the *halakhah* has to be changed, although if there were a way to change it so that a woman could receive a *get* more easily, I would be in favor of it. I do believe that Jewish law comes from God, and the process of changing *halakhah* is difficult. I am convinced that the problem is not so much changing the law as it is making Jews act more as a community.

In a cohesive Jewish community, Jews could join in pressuring a recalcitrant husband to give his wife a *get*. The rabbi might notify him that he is no longer eligible for honors at the *shul*, others might join together to ostracize him. But let's face it, we're not living in a *shtetl* any more. If there are seven *shuls* in the

area, a man who is turned away from one *shul* can always go to another. And, if the man is wealthy, he can donate a lot of money to various organizations, so that community leaders will be hesitant about confronting him, if they happen to know the wife is waiting for a *get*.

There were very few people in any position of prominence in the community who could do anything for me while I waited for a *get*. Moral support was what most people offered, but that wasn't all I was looking for. I started a Chicago chapter of the GET organization (Get Equitable Treatment) to work with other women in similar positions, and to make the community aware of the seriousness of the *get* problem. My organization couldn't help me receive a *get* from my ex-husband. I received it only after making personal sacrifices, giving my ex-husband certain custody rights. I had no choice.

Now that women in Chicago have begun working together on this issue, we might be able to achieve more to help one another if we act together. In Toronto, for instance, a group of women refused to go to the *mikvah*—thereby preventing sexual relations with their husbands—until their husbands agreed to pressure a man in the community to give a *get*. That's just one form of power that Jewish women can utilize.

When Jewish women band together to do something good for one another—as well as for the entire community—there is nothing that can stop us. Jewish women have to realize their own power. We are the cornerstone of Judaism.

KHANE FEYGL ABRAHAM
Chicago, Illinois

American Jews are starved for the same thing I was starved for before I became religious—that warm, good feeling of belonging, of knowing who you are and where you are going.

Exodus

My parents taught me only one thing about Judaism: To be proud of being a Jew. This was an amazing gift in the Soviet Union, where many Jews try to hide that fact from their children. There, being called a Jew is like being cursed. Yet my parents taught me to hold my head up high.

In Russia, we had no access to Jewish books. My parents didn't teach me about Jewish history, holidays, or rituals. The only holiday we marked was Passover—and all we could do then was to go to Moscow's only synagogue to buy *matzah*. Since people have been persecuted for their religious beliefs, my parents never talked about God. All they could safely teach me was pride—pride in being a Jew.

My husband Edward and I decided to leave the Soviet Union because we didn't see any future for our children as Jews. We knew they would be unable to get good jobs, and they would never feel part of the society. My husband also felt that he didn't want to give the benefit of all his learning and knowledge to the Soviets. He knew the Soviet system was wrong.

In 1975 we applied for visas, but we were denied. The emigration officials always changed the reasons and the reasons were always illogical. The first time they informed us that we couldn't leave because one of my brothers worked at a company and had access to state secrets. Another time they refused us because of my husband's job in the government's meteorology department. At another time, they simply said that they thought it was unreasonable for us to leave the country.

Once we were denied visas, we became refuseniks. My husband was asked to leave his job by some of his Jewish co-workers. They were afraid that they would be harrassed because of his desire to leave. I had to work to support the family. My co-workers ignored me because they didn't want to appear sympathetic, but the world of other refuseniks suddenly opened up to us. My older son, Alex, began studying Judaism in underground classes, and my husband helped organize the first underground Jewish song festival. I met Ida Nudel and other female activists who gave me hope and encouragement—they were my role models in my fight for freedom.

When you're in refusal, you're nowhere. You're not part of Russian society, yet you're not out of it either. You can't practice your profession, you can't practice your religion, you don't know what might happen to you the next day. At least a prisoner is allowed to know how many years he will spend in prison. A refusenik knows nothing. The whole country becomes a ghetto.

My family and I lived in an atmosphere of impending terror. Whenever I left the house, my children feared never seeing me again; there was no assurance that I would return. We waited four years and then decided the situation had become critical. Alex was about to turn eighteen, which meant he would be drafted at any moment. Once a Soviet citizen serves in the army, he is thought to possess military secrets and is not allowed to leave the country for five to fifteen years. We knew that demonstrations and public activism were our only option—even if it meant living on the razor's edge.

Our exodus out of Russia gave new meaning to the word freedom.

As a woman, I was less likely to be imprisoned than Edward, so I decided that it was up to me to fight publicly. Five other women and I planned a series of all-female demonstrations—one at the Kremlin wall—to stress our situation and to fight for our rights to emigrate. We were followed, bugged, harrassed, and physically beaten. But I was never afraid of the danger I was in. I experienced it as a gift from God that I was unafraid. It was not until we came to America that I began to worry about what would have become of me. During my fight in Russia, I always knew exactly what I was doing and when I had to stop; I knew where their weaknesses lay and how I had to proceed. I always had one goal in front of me: We had to get out of Russia that year. I think my instinct as a mother took over. When you have to protect your children, you do whatever you have to do. Every other feeling disappears.

Our exit in 1978 was an incredible stroke of luck. A cousin in America managed to add our names to a list of some refusenik families that Senator Edward Kennedy demanded be freed when he came to Moscow. Of these, only six families from Moscow got permission to leave, and one of them was ours. When I heard on the Voice of America that we were being released, I cried. I think it was the first time I ever believed in God. Then I asked, "Why us? Other people have waited much longer. Why are we allowed to go?"

I've been in America for almost ten years, but every day I think of the people in refusal. I feel a responsibility to help save the lives of Jews who want to leave the Soviet Union. Their situation is perilous. The best way to work for the refuseniks is to be active in the Jewish community. That's why I'm involved in Jewish organizations here. I want to share my experiences and tell American Jews that Soviet Jews are still in danger. American Jews have a voice here and they can influence the American government—that's something I've learned to appreciate.

Some Jews say that Jews leaving the Soviet Union should go straight to Israel. But to many Russian Jews, being Jewish is like a mark on their bodies that classifies them as second-class citizens. They have no attachment to Israel or to Judaism. They don't want to go to Israel because they've never heard anything positive about it in the Soviet media. All they want is to leave the country. I don't think it matters where they go—as long as they are safely out of the Soviet Union.

When we emigrated, there was only bitterness in our hearts. We felt we needed a period of time in America to become Jews so that if we wanted to go to Israel, we could go there with love. Maybe we're staying here now the way Moses wandered with his people for forty years in the desert. They needed time to get rid of their bitterness. They had to learn how to live as free Jews before they could enter the promised land.

GALINA NIZHNIKOV
Andover, Massachusetts

So many Jews still wait in the Soviet Union. My happiness here is tempered by that knowledge. This feeling never leaves me: only freedom for all will ever be enough.

Emancipation

My grandfather was a slave. He was caught in Africa—maybe Ethiopia—when he was a young boy. He and his brothers and sister were separated from their parents when they were sold to an Englishman who transported them to America. On the boat over here, hundreds of black men, women, and children jumped overboard and drowned.

My grandfather was a Jewish man. He said that he was descended from one of the Israelite tribes that strayed into Africa. He secretly celebrated all the Jewish holidays with wine and crackers. He loved to tell me stories from the Bible. But he couldn't publicize his Judaism, because he was frightened he'd be killed by his Christian owners. They wanted to control every part of their slaves' lives, and they were as much against Jews as they were against blacks. My grandfather acted in public the way the white man said he should, but the only time I saw him in a church was at his own funeral.

My grandfather gave me a strong feeling for Judaism. My grandmother never talked about it, but she did tell us not to eat milk and meat together. I followed what she said, but I didn't know any other Jews when I was growing up, so I couldn't practice my religion. When I was about twenty-five, I left North Carolina for New York. I started working as a cook for the Eisenberg family. I worked for them for twenty-four years, nine months, and four days. Mrs. Eisenberg made me feel right at home. She was a religious Jew who accepted me as a Jew and as her equal.

I started going to school to learn more about Judaism and I began to observe Jewish customs. People kept asking me how I had gotten to be Jewish. I didn't want there to be doubt in anyone's mind about who I was, so I had an Orthodox conversion. I didn't feel any different after I left the *mikvah*. I've always felt like a Jew.

People sometimes tell me that they've never seen a black Jew before. I reply that God created only two people and out of those two people came all the different races. I'm not a preacher, but I think that means that we are all brothers and we are all equal.

Black Christians also ask me why I practice Judaism. They think that you don't have religion unless you jump around and shout about it. But my grandfather taught me that religion is how you feel inside and how you live it. Judaism has sweetened up my life.

Freedom. That's what being Jewish has given me. When I was growing up, I had to go through the back door, I couldn't go to a theater or restaurant or say what I wanted to say. But once I came up north and started to live as a Jew, I felt like I was someone. Now I can go anywhere with anyone I want—I'm no longer Jim Crowed. I won't back up for nobody and I don't have to hide my face.

ROSETTA BUGGS
Queens, New York

I believe in the miracle of Hanukkah. Miracles help me believe that I can do anything I want to do.

143

Service

When people asked me what I wanted to be when I grew up, I always said, "A rabbi." They thought it was cute—at that time there was no such thing as a female rabbi—but no one told me I couldn't do it. To me, being a rabbi seemed like a natural thing for a woman to do.

My role models were my Hebrew school teachers. They were Hebrew Union College rabbinical students—some were women by then—who gave me the impression that Judaism was "cool," even avant-garde. They were all against the Vietnam War, and they explained why this war was against Jewish principles. I developed strong negative feelings about the military from that experience.

My husband, Steven, is also a rabbi; when we went to Israel to study for a year, I thought we would be disturbed by all the young people carrying guns there. But I saw that they weren't pointing guns at anyone, they were defending their country. I saw their strength and pride, and that seemed healthy to me.

Once we returned home, Steven and I realized that we lacked a tangible commitment to this country. All we have to do is pay taxes, and that didn't seem like much compared to all we received. We felt that we'd taken advantage of America, but that we hadn't been giving anything back in return.

We didn't wake up one morning and decide to become chaplains in the military, but when we heard about the chaplaincy as a summer job, it sounded interesting to us. The Navy would pay us to learn counseling and administrative skills, and we would have the opportunity to do some ecumenical work without any obligations to serve further. We thought we would have an enjoyable summer experience. Once we were involved, though, we saw the problems that Jews face in the military.

Two percent of the Navy is Jewish, a figure that mirrors the percentage of Jews in the country. But out of 1,100 Navy chaplains, only 12 are Jewish, which means that most Jews go through their entire military career without seeing a rabbi in uniform. They see priests taking care of Catholics, Protestant chaplains taking care of Protestants, but there's no rabbi taking care of them. It's a very lonely feeling. During our summer there, service people were so excited when they saw the little pins we wore—the Ten Commandments with a Jewish star over them—that they broke rank just to speak to us. It made us think about doing a three-year stint in the Navy after we graduated from rabbinical school.

I applied to the Jewish Welfare Board for sponsorship to the Navy. I had graduated from chaplaincy school with all As, and scored as a first-class marine on the physical fitness test, yet the board refused to endorse me. I knew the Orthodox board members might have trouble endorsing a female rabbi, but the JWB's vote didn't have to be unanimous.

I waited and waited. Finally, a few weeks before I was supposed to begin service, I officially asked the Reform movement's Central Conference of American Rabbis to endorse me on its own so that the Navy could hire me.

I have small, beautiful dreams for myself.

Suddenly I was in the midst of a controversy. People said the Jewish Welfare Board was the one organization in which rabbis of all denominations work together—and I had disrupted it. But since that incident, each denomination can endorse its own rabbis—under the aegis of the JWB.

I was never a "first" in anything until this happened. Now I understand why the first women who open doors can be angry or bitter. It's very hard being a first—people are constantly watching me to make sure I don't slip up. As the Navy's only female Jewish chaplain, I feel that every time I do something it has to be especially good. At the same time, I have to be one of the boys because I'm surrounded by men.

People ask me how I can be part of the war machine. I explain that my feelings about the military haven't changed: As a Jew, I am a pursuer of peace. But, unfortunately, this world requires armies; to think otherwise is unrealistic. And contrary to what some think, the people in the military are not warmongers. They're the ones whose lives are on the line. I've never heard an officer talking about going to war without also saying, "Let's hope this never happens" or "God forbid."

As a chaplain, my role is to minister to people, which really means caring for people. Non-Jewish people come in and ask for my help too, and I can offer them the religious support they need. I sometimes help people get around the Navy's bureaucratic red tape, I organize a discussion group for people who

test positive for AIDS, and I'm there for any other problems that might come up. Jewish teaching emphasizes social action and helping one's neighbors—that is the main focus of my job on a daily basis.

When I counsel, I counsel from a female point of view; at the same time, I'm a rabbi. Since I'm a wife, I can counsel with a wife's perspective, and when I become a mother, I'm sure that will affect how I see things too. I'm probably more nurturing than male rabbis; in my sermons, for instance, I emphasize support and caring more than large political themes.

Military people often ask me why they never see any other Jews in the military. I explain that there aren't that many Jews in America, but the truth is, I'm embarrassed that more Jews don't serve. It's partially socioeconomic—Jews are trained to go to college and become professionals, like other middle-class kids. But if American Jews don't participate in the military, it will reinforce the stereotypes that Jews don't give of themselves and they're not part of the mainstream.

I'm in the Navy to help Jews who serve in the military. I also want to contribute to America. I am repaying the debt for all America has given to me—as well as to other Jews. I'm not just living here. There's something about wearing my uniform that says I am part of this country.

JULIE SCHWARTZ
Oakland, California

I still don't salute smartly and crisply, the way a marine would. I feel like I'm flicking flies out of my hair. The first time I saluted, I felt I was dressed up in a costume and pretending. It was similar to the first time people called me "Rabbi"—I couldn't believe they were talking to me.

Sanctuary

When I read an article about Central American refugees' treacherous journey to the United States, I knew then that I had to help them. I discovered that women are raped, children kidnapped, and men assaulted and robbed. Once they arrive in this country, they're forced to hide like criminals. I felt a sense of urgency; I couldn't ignore their plight.

After leaving my job at a Jewish social service agency in Madison, I went to work for over two years with the Sanctuary movement in the Rio Grande Valley, Texas. The area is on the border of Mexico and hundreds of refugees pass through there each week. I helped to provide them with food, shelter, medical attention, and legal advice.

All the volunteers did what they could to help the refugees. When I found out, for example, that nuns were the only people allowed to visit refugees in jail, I began to identify myself as a nun when it was necessary. I removed my jewelry and make-up, dressed in a white blouse and plain skirt, and wore a cross lent to me by a nun. I was then allowed into restricted areas. I grew accustomed to being called "sister" by people who didn't know me. As soon as I finished my work, however, I took off the cross. I wasn't uncomfortable, but I sensed the responsibility of wearing the symbol of another people's religion.

The nuns I worked with inspired me with their courage and faith. They, as well as other Christians, explained how the Sanctuary movement has been influenced by the Old Testament's emphasis on justice, economic equality, and communalism. During services with the refugees, people read Old Testament passages about helping a stranger in your midst, or protecting those who flee from persecution. I saw how easily the refugee workers could relate to the Judaic laws of gleaning—farmers should always leave a portion of their harvest for the poor—or the concept of the Jubilee Year—every fifty years slaves should be freed and land redistributed. I had always believed in such communal tenets before I became involved with Sanctuary, but I never realized how these biblical mandates would serve to justify my work for human rights.

I was drawn to working with the refugees because I, too, have felt like a displaced person. Although I was born in the United States, I felt marginal in the Milwaukee neighborhood where I grew up. It lacked tumult, a sense of ethnicity, and substance. I felt alienated from it and thought of living in another country. I moved to Israel to put down roots.

The hardest part about living in Israel was the contradictory sensations I felt. I was nationalistic, yet I had trouble accepting the way Israelis treated the Palestinians. I felt sympathetic to the Palestinian cause because I recognized their feeling of homelessness—an issue that already absorbed me. I became friends with a Palestinian man and we tried to work together toward change, but it was very difficult. We were forced to meet in secret because my Israeli Jewish friends could not accept him. Our friendship gradually ended. Later I was told that he had joined the Palestinian group Al Fatah.

I knew even then that people without a home were people I wanted to work with. I wanted to help them

My husband and I invited a family of Guatemalan refugees to celebrate Passover with us. The Passover story is very real for them. They have experienced oppression firsthand. Redemption to them means returning to their homeland—only nobody can say when that will be.

and—although I wasn't aware of this at the time—I wanted to resolve my own feelings of rootlessness. I came to this understanding in Israel, but I didn't feel I could do this work in Israel because separation from my family and friends had become difficult. I moved back to the States, and started to work with refugees from the Soviet Union and Indochina.

When I became active in leftist movements, I found myself, once again, divided by contradictory alliances. Whenever I tried to articulate how my political ideas were linked to my Jewish beliefs, people labeled me a Zionist, too idealistic or overly emotional. I have always struggled to express myself in relation to my religion and culture as a whole Jew allied with the political left.

I continued to feel dislocated in this way until I joined the Sanctuary movement. The year I worked in Texas, I met people who reminded me that the United States was formed by hard work, struggle, a commitment to justice, and clarity of vision. They helped me "discover America," and it made me realize that this country can speak to me in an important way. Now that I'm back in Madison and working for the Sanctuary movement on a grass-roots level, I finally feel attached to a community, as well as to this country and its history.

I still haven't entirely resolved the question of how to maintain integrity, confidence, and pride as a Jew while at the same time remain concerned with problems of the general secular community. This duality may never be resolved—perhaps that's one of the complexities of being a Jew. But I've been able to fuse the personal, political, and religious components of my life into my Sanctuary work. I've found people who encourage me to contribute my ideas about my faith in the work we do. They celebrate with me just as I've learned to celebrate with them.

Many Jews have told me that they don't think the Sanctuary movement is a Jewish concern. Since the refugees are Catholic, they reason, Catholics should take care of them. But their rationalization is the equivalent of Christians saying they didn't have to help Jewish refugees during World War II because they were Jews. In fact, the religion of refugees doesn't matter. If we hear the voice of the oppressed and we turn away from that voice, then we are shirking our responsibility as Jews. Jewish tradition reminds us that by saving the life of one person, you are saving the whole world.

LAURIE LEMEL
Madison, Wisconsin

For some women, the awareness of being Jewish is sudden; for others, it is a slow, often ambivalent process. Finding a comfortable Jewish identity is a series of revelations that illuminate a woman's life, her outlook, and her relationship to the world. A woman's discovery of her Jewishness and what it means to her often leads to other questions: What is my place within a historical Jewish context? What prayers and rituals can I use to express my spirituality and how do I share what I've learned with others? The resolutions of these issues inspire other women to continue on their own paths of transformation and renewal.

DISCOVERIES

Choice

Montana is the true Diaspora. There is one synagogue—Reform—in the entire state. A student rabbi flies in from Cincinnati every other week to conduct Sabbath services, and when he's not there, we have to do everything ourselves. If my husband and I want to learn about Judaism, we have to search out the books, we have to do the reading. We have to be more committed than Jews who live in large Jewish communities, with many Jewish resources: We have to pursue our Jewish studies ourselves. We have no one else to rely on.

Before I met my husband, Brian, I had never even met a Jew before. I was like most other people in Montana—I didn't know what Judaism was. One night after we started dating, Brian told me, "I have something to confess to you." I assumed he was going to tell me something obscene. He said, "I'm Jewish." My response was, "Is that all? What is there to be ashamed of? And why is it such a secret?" He told me about the synagogue in Billings, and I suggested that we go there together. I found the services comforting; I could relate to the prayers. I began taking classes with the rabbi.

I studied Judaism seriously for four years. Brian and I were living together, and we discussed getting married after I converted. I don't think I would have converted to Judaism if I hadn't met Brian, but I didn't want to convert just to please Brian or his family. I wanted to do it for myself.

Yet when I talked to the rabbi about my conversion, he told me that he was willing to perform the ceremony and sign the paper the following month. I would have liked him to tell me to study Torah for a year, or to learn to read Hebrew. I was preparing earnestly for my conversion, and I was disappointed that the Reform movement seemed to take it so casually. I didn't want an Orthodox conversion because I knew I couldn't live the life of an Orthodox Jew, but I appreciate how the Orthodox turn down potential converts three times. They want to make sure that conversion is truly desired. I knew it was what I wanted.

The more I learned about Judaism, the more I found that the religion enriched my life. It gave me a new understanding of morality, as well as a sensitivity toward things I had never thought about before. Brian and I used to hunt, for example; the only meat we ate was from animals that we had killed ourselves. But one time I injured an animal in the back leg and I could see the pain I had caused. I ran after it, trying to kill it, and I realized then that Jews eat kosher meat so that the animal is killed quickly and does not suffer. After that incident I stopped hunting. The Jewish teaching of respect for other living creatures was suddenly important to me.

Gradually, Brian and I decided to follow more and more Jewish observances. We took them on in stages because it made our decisions more significant. We also felt that if we took too much upon ourselves all at once, we might have said, "This is overwhelming," and given up. The first year we decided to stop eating milk with meat. That was really challenging for me because I love junk food—I couldn't even eat Kentucky Fried Chicken because it has milk fried into

Brian and I go to the rifle range for target practice; it's a hobby. But some Montana Jews carry guns because they are very vulnerable to the neo-Nazis in nearby Idaho. We've received idle threats on the synagogue's answering machine, but I don't feel personally threatened as a Jew. I do carry a pistol in my car, though, because I'm vulnerable as a woman. Out here, a lot of women are taught how to use weapons to protect ourselves.

the coating. Then we decided to abstain from pork products. That meant asking about the ingredients in every dish at a Chinese restaurant. I still find myself lying, saying, "I'm allergic to pork," because if I were to say, "I'm kosher," no one would understand.

I find it difficult to explain these dietary laws—they might seem archaic to some people. A good friend of mine, for instance, teased me because I didn't want to share her pepperoni pizza. I told her that these laws are commanded of me, they provide me with a regimen, they help keep me—as a Jew—separate and distinct. They serve as a reminder that I'm different.

There are some Jews in Billings who would choose to give up that sense of being different. They think being Christian is more desirable than being Jewish. They have Christmas trees, for example, in order to be like everyone else. They don't disown their Judaism, but they'd prefer to keep it a secret. They assume that because I was born a Lutheran, I grew up on the greener side of the fence. I think the opposite is true. I used to dread getting up on Sunday mornings to go to church and observe my religion for an hour. Now, I wake up every morning and know that I'm a Jew. There isn't a day that goes by that I'm not

reminded. I have stability in my life because I'm living Judaism on a daily basis—not just once a week. My life seems much more precious now.

My Hebrew name is Tamar bat Avraham—Tamar, the daughter of Abraham. All Jews by choice are considered children of Abraham; they're given that name when they convert. When I signed the *ketubbah*—our marriage contract—I was aware that people would always know I'm a Jew by choice because of my name. That's a little threatening to me—I don't always want to be known as a convert. It makes me want to try harder to prove that I'm just as Jewish as the person sitting next to me in synagogue who was born a Jew.

That's why I chose not to have a party after my conversion—I didn't want my transition from non-Jew to Jew to be so public. Although it was a major event in my life, the decision was very personal. I couldn't share it with anyone. I also didn't want to make an announcement: Starting July 10, I am a Jew. I felt Jewish a long time ago.

TAMMIE REITER
Billings, Montana

154

Spark

My mother's family came to America from Kiev one hundred years ago. There were six sisters and they all married non-Jewish men. One of my great aunts joked that the reason they were all unhappy was because they all married Gentiles.

I always figured that if my great-grandmother was Jewish, then my grandmother was half-Jewish, my mother one-quarter Jewish, and I was one-eighth Jewish. My father is Scottish, so I thought of myself as a mixture of these different backgrounds.

I lived in a non-Jewish sorority for a year and I truly felt a sense of sisterhood. The other girls tried very hard not to hurt my feelings. They felt so uncomfortable saying the word "Jew" that they would almost whisper it. Finally, I told them, "You can say the word out loud, it's not taboo!"
(*Sherry Manning, far right*)

When I was about thirteen, my grandmother died and my grandfather, who happened to have been Jewish, remarried an observant Jewish woman. The first time she met my sister and me, she asked us how Jewish we thought we were. I said, "An eighth," and she said, "No. If your great-grandmother was Jewish, that means your grandmother, mother, and you are all Jews." She paused and then said, "Not only that, but your children will be 100 percent Jewish."

What she said changed my life. I felt as if a special gift had been given to me. My being Jewish didn't feel like my choice, but God's. I was a member of the Jewish people, and that identity would be passed on to my children—it would not end with me.

Suddenly, I was Jewish, but I didn't know anything about Judaism. I had always celebrated Christmas and Easter with my family, and I went to church often with my father. The Methodist faith was the only religion I knew. But none of that bothered me.

I started studying Judaism on my own. I wanted to attend services at a synagogue, but I felt shy. I used to drive past synagogues in Kansas City, but I was too timid to stop the car and go inside. I was apprehensive about people asking me what I was doing there, felt they might think that I didn't belong. Finally, my father asked a Jewish woman in his office if she would go with me to services. She agreed.

That first Friday evening was overwhelming. I loved being surrounded by other Jews. All I did was ask questions: Why does the prayer book open backwards? What does it mean to be a Zionist? Why does the rabbi wear a shawl? I felt like I had to catch up on all the knowledge that other Jews my age take for granted.

My mother is glad that I've taken Judaism seriously—she's even begun hinting that I should marry a Jewish man. At first my father thought it was a good idea for me to learn about my Jewish heritage. Although he's had some mixed feelings about my decision to practice Judaism, he now accepts it.

I still celebrate Christmas with him and the rest of my family, but I also celebrate Jewish holidays on my own. I want my father to understand that I am not rejecting him or his non-Jewish background by choosing to live as a Jew. My commitment to Judaism has increased my desire to learn about our Scottish heritage as well. Now I joke that I'm a Celtic Jew; it's a humorous way for me to reconcile my two distinct identities.

That's why I'm also not as upset about intermarriage as some other Jews seem to be. I feel that Judaism can be synthesized with other cultures. For example, once when I heard a rabbi condemn marriages between Jews and non-Jews, I raised my hand and said, "My Mom is Jewish and my Dad isn't, but they're both good people and they love each other. I don't see how that could be wrong." I would prefer to marry a Jewish man, but if I fall in love with a Gentile, I will marry him. He'll have to respect my beliefs, however, and agree to let me raise our children as Jews.

Judaism isn't necessarily lost when Jewish women marry non-Jews. My mother's family may not have pursued Judaism, but they never converted to any other religion. They still had what people call the *pintele Yid,* a Jewish spark that remained inside them. I rediscovered that spark by accident, and now I want to incorporate Judaism into my life and my future.

SHERRY MANNING
Lawrence, Kansas

Visibility

I grew up in a working-class Jewish home in the Bronx. My father owned and drove a taxicab. Although we had enough food, a place to live, and warm clothes, my parents struggled with the feeling of not being "good enough" and with the fear of being poor. They fought a lot about money and material needs. I don't know whether they fought about money so often because they didn't like each other and that was just one of their problems, or if they didn't like one another because they each had a different way of dealing with money, survival, and fear. I always felt like we weren't as good or as worthy as

I have too often felt "other." I've been treated by straight middle-class Jews as though I am not the right kind of Jew; I've been treated by other working-class people as though being Jewish and working-class are diametrically opposed conditions. But here I am in the flesh, climbing out of all those stereotypes!

the other families in our neighborhood. Their fathers stayed home on the High Holy Days, but my father couldn't afford to take time off—for many years he worked seven days a week. I didn't feel as worthy as the little girls on my block who wore fancy dresses, or whose families drove nice cars. I always felt a lot of fear, anger, and pain about material failure and lack of self-esteem.

I wasn't aware of the issues of class differences until my late twenties, when I started to understand that class not only has to do with money but is also about respect, expectations, and self-worth. I began to acknowledge that I'm working class and to understand its significance in my life. At the same time, my involvement in the lesbian community helped me learn to deal with other forms of privilege and oppression.

Slowly I realized that trying to look, act, and sound like white, middle-class, Christian America—assimilating—is self-hating. A woman once said to me, "What's wrong with assimilation is that we are trying to be like someone else. Why aren't they trying to be like us?" Click—I got it. I was aware that my Jewishness was another part of my identity that I had pushed away in the desire to be someone else, to be someone "more acceptable."

My father had changed his name from Rabinowitz to Gordon; my mother had changed her name from Arianna to Anne; they named me Donna Susan. Everything that was obviously Jewish had been stripped away from me, and the more being Jewish became important to me, the more uncomfortable I became with my name. I felt that I wanted to become visible as a Jew, the way I had taken a public stand about

being lesbian and being working class. I wanted to be true to myself and not hide behind a name that would help me assimilate. I didn't need to prove that I was Jewish, but I did want to take a Jewish name that reflected my new sense of pride in my identity. I asked my mother what my Hebrew name was. She couldn't remember, so I took the name of Dvora, which is the closest Hebrew equivalent of Donna.

Oy, so what is being Jewish about? I've thought about this question for a long time. For me, Jewishness is about humor, questioning, survival, ancestry, and noise. Noise? Yes, being loud. Talking loud, laughing loud, arguing loud, being alive and loud about being alive. And humor—for the fun of it and for survival, because you can survive anything if you can keep a sense of humor. Being Jewish is being part of a people who have survived Egyptian slavery, Russian pogroms, Spanish inquests, the Holocaust—and we're still alive, challenging, laughing, and fighting. We never accept things "just because," whether it's an issue that concerns politics, religion, or something personal. It's searching for the truth and for what feels right.

It seems my life has been a series of unravelings about who I am and what I believe as someone who is working class, a lesbian, a Jew. I continue to grow and to change all the time, discovering new aspects of my identity. This is who I am now; but as Alice says in Wonderland, "I knew who I was when I woke up this morning, but I seem to have changed many times since."

DVORA GORDON
Oakland, California

I used to go from job to job. I drove delivery vans, did clerical work at a library, washed cars. For the past four years I've been doing gardening work, so now I can say, "I'm a gardener." But I try not to identify myself in this way. Too much attention, respect, and sense of worth is focused on what you do to make money, and not on who you really are.

Mainstream

I don't have any portraits of my great-grandparents; I've never heard any family legends. I know my grandparents came from Russia, Poland, and Germany, but that's all I know. I assume that if I could trace my family back far enough, we'd surface somewhere in the Middle East. I don't feel like a direct descendant of Rachel, Rebecca, and Leah, however. It's as if my family sprung up from a pit on the Lower East Side of Manhattan, and then moved to Long Island.

The neighborhood where I grew up was very new. The trees were small, the houses were still being built, and everything felt transient. I had no sense of history or continuity. No one I knew ever talked much about our Jewish heritage, but I was still curious about it. I wanted to have a Jewish education but I was denied. My father has always said that he is a cultural Jew and that the religion doesn't interest him. On Hanukkah, he put an electric menorah in the window so that other people would know that he was Jewish and kept the faith. But we never lit the candles nor discussed the meaning of the holiday.

I grew up thinking that being Jewish meant shopping in malls, hating nature, and talking about non-Jews as "the *goyim*"; I thought it meant going to college to get a good job and earn a lot of money. The Jews I knew seemed very shallow and materialistic. I thought that being a young Jewish woman meant being a Jewish American Princess, and being an older Jewish woman meant marrying a short dumpy man and playing mah-jongg. Since I didn't feel like either kind of woman, I thought there was no place for me among Jews. Those stereotypes chased me away from Judaism.

I associated so many negative qualities with Long Island Jews that I couldn't wait to leave. In college, I was glad my blond hair and blue eyes prevented me from looking Jewish. I wouldn't wear nail polish, because I was frightened people would call me a JAP. I had some Jewish friends, but I was more interested in associating with people from other countries. After college, I worked in London for a year; then I returned to the States and moved to Virginia, where I met my husband, Rees Tate Bowen VII.

Rees is a very calm, stable man who raises and sells cattle. He grew up in the farmhouse where his family has lived since the 1700s. The Bowens talk about their ancestors so often that it is as though all of the generations are still around. His family is connected to their history and the role they played in the founding of this country.

When I married Rees, I felt like I entered into mainstream America. His family seems like landed gentry. Rees isn't rich or ambitious, but he is super-American. Marrying him was almost my family's way of saying, "We have all arrived."

The Bowens represent an aspect of American life that I always felt excluded from. Their family seems like one you'd find on television or in a Norman Rockwell painting. Although I never cared before about clubs that they joined and I couldn't, I am now secretly tickled that a daughter I might have could become a member of the Daughters of the American Revolution. I must admit that I'm happy my future son will be called Rees Bowen VIII. I like the idea of being a chameleon who can blend in with others.

I wasn't brought up to believe in God and I think that's a lack in my life. I'm trying to develop a religious feeling inside—faith—because it seems comforting. My husband isn't a practicing Christian but he's a very religious man in his own way. He always tells me, "I'm a farmer and I ain't never seen nothing come from nothing."

Once I married Rees, and started to feel comfortable with his family and friends, I felt triumphant. I was finally accepted by WASPs, who had always held a certain mystique for me. I learned how to set a table properly, to be a gracious hostess, and to make Jello salads as well as the right conversation at Christmas parties. Even with these skills, however, I still feel different from the Bowens, maybe because of the values I subconsciously learned on Long Island—the same values I used to ridicule.

I'm much more interested in education and learning than the Bowens and their friends are; I seem to be the only one concerned with giving to charity and taking an active role in helping other people. And although my family always seemed too emotionally involved with one another, I feel that Rees and his family don't talk enough about their personal feelings.

Ironically, being away from a sizable Jewish community has given me a deeper appreciation of both the cultural and religious aspects of Judaism. I no longer think it's so terrible that Jewish kids are brainwashed to go to college; it's a way to be self-supporting and to make something of oneself. Having money doesn't seem horrible either; it buys freedom, and the more you have, the more you can give away to charities. There are only one hundred Jews in Bluefield, but they seem to be the best and brightest people in the community. They are intellectuals, they're doers, they head many of the volunteer organizations, they're well traveled, they're compassionate. There must have been people like them on Long Island—I didn't see them.

When I first moved down here, I was surprised to discover that there were any Jews in the area. I went to the temple out of curiosity. I expected to find the religion to be a lot of mumbo-jumbo, but it has great wise teachings about justice, charity, community, and God that make a lot of sense to me.

I became more involved with the Jewish congregation here because I wanted to connect with the Jewish religion. Being far enough away from Long Island enabled me to strip away many images and cultural stereotypes I had held about Jews, and I was able to turn to the Torah, to a belief in one God, and to Judaism itself.

Part of what has allowed me to discover my own belief in Judaism is my own growth and maturing—including an emotional separation from my family and whatever pain and disappointments they might have caused me. Over the last few years, I have been able to forgive them, so I no longer feel the need to carve out a life that's focused on being different from them.

Now I can smile at my father's brand of cultural Judaism—which means being in a place where he can buy bagels on Sunday morning—and not feel so threatened by those Long Island Jews whose values don't match mine. Letting go of this bitterness has helped free me to find a religious Jewish identity for myself. I do not know what the future has in store for me—I'm thinking of leaving Virginia and I'm not sure if Rees will come with me—but I do know that my discovery of Judaism has finally enabled me to embrace myself as a Jew, and to feel a part of the Jewish people.

MELODY BOWEN
Tazewell, Virginia

I don't think Rees will convert to Judaism, but he has agreed to raise our children Jewish. Still, I think it will be difficult for any children we might have. Not only will all their relatives be Christian, but there are so few Jewish children in this area. At least in an area with a lot of Jews, children can learn to be Jewish by osmosis; they pick up Yiddish words, for example. It seems strange that my kids might talk about carrying something heavy and never say *shlep*.

Search

I feel like a stranger to Judaism. My parents always wanted to assimilate. Even though they moved to a New York suburb that was predominantly Jewish, they were ambivalent about their Judaism, and I grew up feeling I had no identity at all. It's only now that I've begun to be interested in Judaism—but I'm still confused about how much of the religion I want in my life.

I was pregnant with my first child when I began to think about what being Jewish meant to me. If I had a boy, I didn't know whether to circumcise him. Everything in me said no—it's an unnecessary and traumatic operation—but a small voice in my head reminded me that I didn't know any Jewish men who weren't circumcised. My father told me, "If you don't circumcise him, I won't be able to think of him as my grandson." I asked him why, but he couldn't explain his feelings. I was surprised that both my father and I were experiencing such a deep, subconscious connection to Judaism.

I wanted to find a rabbi with whom I could discuss my conflict—so I looked for a synagogue in the Yellow Pages! I didn't expect to find one in the Napa Valley, but I did. The rabbi I contacted was accessible and supportive. He didn't say, "You must circumcise your son," but he did explain the reasons why Jews perform circumcision. At the same time, he gave me the name of a group that opposes the practice. After much soul-searching I decided that I would circumcise my son—but I was secretly relieved when my daughter was born instead.

The rabbi invited me to attend the services he conducts with a Reconstructionist congregation. I was nervous because I thought I would feel out of place. I had little knowledge of Jewish traditions, history, and culture, with the exception of the occasional bar mitzvahs I had attended—and disliked—when I was growing up. Yet I didn't feel intimidated at the first service. It was comforting to see how the community welcomed non-Jewish spouses as members—my ignorance about Judaism made me feel like a non-Jew.

I started attending services regularly, and the more I learned about Reconstructionist ideas, the more they appealed to me. I appreciated that Reconstructionism grants full equality to women and that it stresses Judaism's need to evolve in modern society. Tradition is taken seriously, but Judaism has a vote, not a veto, in one's life. To me, that means that we should know what the doctrines are but we don't have to follow every law.

My husband often comes to services with me. I don't expect Kris to convert to Judaism, but I'm grateful for his support and agreement to raise our children as Jews. I've always felt a spiritual connection to God; now I want that feeling within a more traditional Jewish framework. Yet this sometimes fills me with conflicting emotions; I don't know how to perform any of the rituals. I've tried following a "How to do Shabbat" sheet that the rabbi gave me. The prayers are written out phonetically and I feel silly trying to read them out loud. Kris and I sometimes light one candle on Friday night—not the customary two—

In the years I've worked at Inglenook Vineyards in the Napa Valley, I've been virtually surrounded by a sea of crosses. I've felt very comfortable here, but now, I'm slightly ashamed that I have so easily assimilated. It wasn't until just recently that I've begun to identify myself as a Jew.

and we've made a roast chicken, but that's as far as we've gone for now.

I want to retrieve some kind of Jewish identity. I think that's why I named my second daughter Sophie, after my father's mother. She came from Russia, she spoke only Yiddish, and it always saddened me that my father seemed embarrassed by her. But she reminds me of what my ancestors must have been like—a foreign, salt-of-the-earth woman from a heritage that I know nothing about. In a way, I gave my daughter her name to backtrack, to grab onto something that was lost. But I don't know yet what it is.

BARB LANG
Rutherford, California

Prayer

When I was in first grade, I learned that Hashem created the world. I was fascinated when the teacher explained how at first there was *nishtikeyt*—nothingness—and then God fashioned something new each day. I loved the concept; I believed in it.

I've always had a great commitment to Judaism. I've chosen to say morning prayers every day, even though as a woman I am not obligated. Jewish law says that women are supposed to thank God at some point during the day, in any language, but they are not required to say the traditional prayers three times a day the way men are. The souls of both men and women need nourishment through daily prayer.

I like to pray in the morning. I like to use a prayerbook and to recite prayers that Jews have repeated for thousands of years. The written prayers are more meaningful to me than anything I could make up on my own. The Hebrew words have a holiness in themselves; they are windows through which God peeks into our hearts.

Praying is like practicing the piano: The more you do it, the better you get at it. I always try to concentrate on what I'm saying, but there are many moments when my mind wanders and I think about my work rather than the prayers. What I try to do is enclose myself in my own world. A man puts on a *tallit* to wrap himself in his prayer, to remove himself from the material world. I don't wear a *tallit*, but similarly, I try to cut myself off so I'm not aware of what is going on around me. Even when I *daven* on the subway I try to find inspiration out of the depths.

Some people object to the fact that Orthodox Jewish men say a prayer in the morning in which they thank God for not making them women. The men's blessing doesn't bother me. Some people say that men say this prayer because they are grateful that they have more religious commandments to fulfill, an explanation I find too simplistic. Psychologists say that some people raise their self-esteem by putting other people down—but I don't think that men feel better about themselves by saying this prayer. I'm not sure why the prayer was worded that way, but I'm sure it was written for an important spiritual purpose—I don't think it is meant to demean women.

When I pray, I don't concentrate on the blessing men say; instead, I meditate on the prayer women are supposed to say. We thank God for creating us "according to His will," and that seems like a much greater compliment to us. The men thank God for not making them women but we thank God for making us the way we are. A positive statement is always much stronger than a negative one. Our prayer might also imply that women are created more in the image of God. Hashem is the epitome of sensitivity, and women are more sensitive than men. The prayer implies that our nature—what motivates us—is more similar to God's than is the nature of men.

There are many places in the Gemara, the book of Oral Law, that group women with slaves and children. This doesn't mean that Judaism views men as superior beings, nor does it mean that the great Jewish scholars saw women as inferior to men. Every great Jewish man respected women. When Isaac and

Ishmael were fighting and Sarah wanted to send Ishmael away, God told Abraham, "Listen to your wife." Abraham did what Sarah said. Jews recognize that women sometimes have better intuition and a more accurate understanding of what is going on.

I don't feel that there should be a dichotomy between secular and religious life. I feel that a Jew is an integrated individual; I try to make Judaism pervade every fiber of my being and everything I do.

Some of my friends feel that since they live in a Jewish neighborhood and since they spend Shabbes with family and friends, they don't need to feel Jewish in their workplace. I do. I like working in an office with other Jews, even if they're not religious. I like to hear people talk about what they did on Rosh Hashannah, or ask how the fast was on Yom Kippur. Those small conversations are important to the texture and quality of my life.

When I've interviewed for accounting jobs, I've always said right away that I leave early for Shabbes. I like to tell people before I'm hired for a job, since accountants often work overtime on Shabbes during tax season. I have to make up the work another time. I'd rather warn future employers in advance; if they don't want to hire me because I'm observant, I'd understand.

My career is very important to me but Judaism is my priority. My life often seems like a roller coaster—I work during the day and go to law school four evenings a week—and Shabbes reminds me that there's more to life than just working. An aquaintance once told me, "Shabbes is a time to walk in the rain slowly; to smell a flower; to ask the questions you forgot all week. Shabbes is a time to forget the ache that wouldn't go away."

Fortunately, I've never had a conflict, or experienced negative reactions to my observance. People are respectful of my beliefs. My friends in the office have even learned to recognize the symbol for *kashrut* on food—they buy kosher cookies so that I can eat them, too.

Friday mornings in the office have a special aura, an *erev Shabbes* atmosphere. That special feeling accompanies me as I leave the office early on Friday afternoon and take the subway home to Brooklyn. The train is always filled with other observant Jews, many of them reading Jewish books. We are all traveling home for the same reason. Sometimes, when I'm working hard at the office and it's getting late, a colleague who might have known nothing about Shabbes before he met me will say, "Go home already, the sun is going down."

JUDITH KRAMER
Brooklyn, New York

When I'm late for work, I *daven* on the subway. It doesn't matter where I pray. God is everywhere. There is no place where He is not.

Irony

My parents' generation tried to escape the *shtetl*. They wanted to leave their Jewish roots and move into a split-level house with a backyard near a shopping mall. That was the American dream. And it's sad, in a way, because it's as if they were put into a Cuisinart with other ethnic groups and blended into some sort of processed American paste.

I'm a product of this environment and I've rebelled against it. I don't find the shopping malls beautiful—they seem soulless to me. I've tried to put more substance into my life. Some people find that substance by returning to Jewish observance; I've found it in my work as a filmmaker.

I draw from my childhood experiences in my movies. I made the protagonist, Roberta, in "Desperately Seeking Susan," a Jewish housewife who wanted to change her life. People in middle America might not have known that she was Jewish—I didn't make it too obvious—but I knew who she was. I made her Jewish because I know Jews, and I can make fun of her because I've learned how to make fun of myself.

I've inherited this sense of irony from my father's family. His mother was agnostic. Judaism to her meant being political and intellectual; Jewish traditions were nothing more than superstitions of an older generation. She used to show me pictures of my great-grandmother, who bought her clothes in London and didn't wear a wig like other Jewish women of her time. My grandmother was proud of the fact that her family was modern and not religious.

Yet my father's parents never denied that they were Jews. They wanted to drop Jewish rituals, but they felt a strong attachment to Jewish culture. Since Jews were excluded from every society they lived in, they developed their own culture; it was that culture that infused the personalities of my father's family. They were sharp, ironic, and funny. They had a certain sensibility that came from being outsiders. They were observers, with a distinctly Jewish view of the world.

My mother's mother, on the other hand, was dedicated to Jewish traditions. But since she was poorly educated, she could never explain these rituals to me. I sometimes confused her Jewish observances with superstitions, in which she also believed. For instance, when she was sewing a button onto a dress I was wearing, she'd stick a piece of thread in my mouth. I'd ask her why, and she'd say, "So you shouldn't get stuck with a needle." That didn't make sense to me. Then, when I'd ask her why she lit Friday night candles, she still didn't have an answer that satisfied my curiosity. I assumed that that ritual was also a superstition—like the thread in my mouth—because it was never fully explained to me.

I began to feel that only old-fashioned or uneducated people followed my grandmother's form of Jewish observance. But the so-called "modern" Judaism I saw while growing up didn't appeal to me, either. I called it country-club religion: It seemed that people belonged to a synagogue only because they needed a place to throw their daughter's sweet sixteen party. All the high holidays meant to me was getting a day off from school and wearing a nice dress.

I see Judaism as a huge tree that has been growing for five thousand years. There's a part of me that feels guilty—if I don't pass the religion on, one of its branches will dead-end with me.

170

Since I found suburban Jewish experience unstimulating and I couldn't identify with my grandmother's ritualistic Judaism, I had no positive feelings for my Jewish identity. But as I got older and started questioning where I came from and who I am, I realized that a part of me can relate to the long line of Jews who preceded me. My link to Judaism is the Jewish culture I acquired from my father's side of the family. My personality, my identity as an outsider—even though I grew up in Abingdon, Pennsylvania—and my sense of humor are uniquely Jewish. That's my Jewish heritage.

I feel a sense of obligation toward being Jewish now, and a desire to pass on my awareness. But I can't force myself to observe rituals as a way to preserve Judaism. Instead, I'll pass on Jewish culture through my movies.

Although the characters in my movies are not all Jews—or even overtly Jewish—I feel my films are Jewish. In them, I search for answers that I've been asking myself for years. I could have asked those questions in a religious context—by studying Torah, let's say—but instead, I ask them through art.

The religious and artistic impulse are not that different. Both begin with questions; both are concerned with myths and rituals in life. You question the values and times you live in. I can't say that filmmaking is a cosmic experience for me, but it is my attempt to figure out what I believe in, and to search my soul.

SUSAN SEIDELMAN
New York, New York

Jews have always been outsiders—in Spain, in Eastern Europe, and, to some extent, here in America. One or two generations of feeling comfortable in America can't erase this tradition of being outsiders. It's been embedded in our culture for centuries.

Illumination

I've always been an artist. I've also had a very strong Jewish identity. But it was only when I started creating Jewish art that I was able to pull both sides of myself together.

I was first attracted to making *ketubbot*, marriage contracts, because of the illumination that decorated their borders. I liked the possibility of doing very rich and vibrant artwork around a Jewish text. Then I learned how to do Hebrew calligraphy. It surprised me because the calligraphy work was hypnotic, mystical. For the first time, I felt that my whole being—not only my intuition and intellect—was involved in my art.

A *ketubbah* is a legal document that states a husband's obligations to his wife. I think it's important for women to have one so that they're protected in the event of a divorce or death. But it also gives women a connection to their Jewish heritage: Every Jewish bride since Babylonian times—over 2,000 years ago—has had a *ketubbah*. But the main reason I love making *ketubbot* for people is that it is often the only Jewish artwork they will have in their homes. The Hebrew letters add a sense of Jewishness to the atmosphere of the house. I make a point of designing the illumination around the *ketubbah* to be a reflection of the personalities of the husband and wife.

I wasn't observant when I started making *ketubbot*, but I always treated the contracts with a sense of sacredness. I wouldn't work on a *ketubbah* on Shabbat because that is forbidden—even though I didn't observe the laws of Shabbat for myself. Still, I had a strong Jewish identity and, in a way, I longed for an observant way of life. There seemed to be a joy, a purity, and a spirituality that exuded from the observant people I met. I experimented with Judaism for ten years, comparing the religious world with the secular world. I gradually saw that the secular world had very little to offer me that was substantial, so I committed myself to the religious world.

I made *ketubbot* for a long time as a single woman. Rather than depressing me, my work with engaged couples gave me hope. I gleaned a lot of information about what worked in a marriage and what I should look for in a potential partner. I could also see that people were not coupled arbitrarily—they belonged together—and I always felt that a minor miracle had occurred so that they could meet.

I needed time to feel independent, and gain a strong sense of myself, before I was ready to marry. My father has always been strong and my mother was submissive—I grew up with a very low sense of self-esteem. I didn't want to get married and become Mrs. Blank—only a reflection of who my husband was. It took many years for me to feel like a person in my own right. I'm lucky that I am part of a generation that considers it normal and respectable for a woman to be alone until her mid-thirties. There were also enough single women in the New York Orthodox community so that I didn't feel strange.

After a while, however, I felt my life was stagnating. I was burned out from dating. I felt self-centered and

I don't care that women are not permitted to write a Torah or a *mezuzah*. I am grateful that women are allowed to make *ketubbot* so that I can express myself. Thank God for that!

at the same time very isolated. Although I learned how to express myself artistically, I felt there were certain aspects of myself that could only be brought out through marriage. Art never gave me the opportunity to give of myself the way having a family could. I wanted to develop trust and understanding, to give of myself and fulfill myself in a more complete way. I anticipated establishing a Jewish home and doing what I could to elevate the lives of my husband and children.

When I first met Julius, I didn't think he was the right person for me. But we dated and talked seriously, and I saw how we shared similarities: We were both social and outgoing, we related to the world in the same way, and we had some common goals. After about seven months, we came to the point where we would either break up or get married. I did not want another superficial relationship; yet making the step from dating to marriage was difficult for both of us. We didn't just click together like some people who fall in love at first sight, and we both had to overcome a lot of fears about making a commitment.

Orthodox Jews date for a shorter period of time than people in the secular world. You're not supposed to have sex before marriage, and it's very difficult to have a prolonged relationship with someone you can't touch. That isn't to say sex isn't important. The rabbis caution that if you're not physically attracted to someone, no matter how nice the person is and how compatible you are, the relationship may not work because there is something vital missing.

Orthodox Jews also feel that you should marry a person whom you could grow to love—love really follows the decision to marry. I found this to be true: Once I made a commitment to marry Julius, I became less critical and much more accepting about who he was. I began to see him as a part of me. I read a book by an Orthodox man who said that once you get married, if your husband's foot hurts, for example, the wife should say, "His foot hurts *us*," because you begin to experience the pain of the other. Marriage is a partnership, and the other person becomes an extension of yourself.

In a Jewish marriage, each of the couple is half of the whole. You still function as individuals, but without your partner, you're not complete. You're only complete once you're married. I was content before I was married, but it is true: I was always looking for my other half.

CLAIRE MENDELSON CISS
New York, New York

One of the reasons Jews have survived for so many centuries of difficult situations is that the Jewish home has been considered a castle and the Jewish man the king. The wife devoted herself to creating a little island. No matter how difficult the outside world was, you could walk into a Jewish home and feel at peace.

Survival

I was born in the Warsaw Ghetto during World War II. After my father was killed in the ghetto uprising, my mother took me out of the Catholic orphanage where I had been placed and we went to live in the countryside. My mother had Aryan papers so we were able to pass. After the War, we lived in Sweden and then came to New York in 1949.

I felt alienated from the start, even though we lived in a Jewish community in the Bronx. I really didn't understand Jews, for instance, who didn't speak Yiddish and who went to synagogue. The people I felt most comfortable with—other survivors, Yiddish speakers, socialists, Bundists, and atheists—never went to synagogue; our collective Jewish identity never had anything to do with God. For me, the most vital connection to Jewishness has always been through Yiddish, because it conveys a sense of the culture and history of the people I come from.

In the mid-1970s I found myself teaching Yiddish and, at the same time, working in the lesbian/feminist movement. I was trying to live in two very different worlds without having them overlap. Over time, I withdrew from the Jewish world because of the homophobia I found there, and I stayed more and more in the women's community where I felt comfortable. But I still had no place to rest: I had to confront and deal with anti-Semitism I found in some other women. My working toward an understanding of Jewish issues in the women's community pushed me, once again, back into the Jewish world. I soon realized that if I was fighting for the Jewish community, then I had to be accepted by other Jews. I had to change

my approach; I could no longer keep the two worlds apart.

Until the stigma disappears, I have to keep raising gay issues at Jewish functions. I know of parents who are deeply ashamed of and angry at their gay children. There are gays who are silent because they fear rejection by their parents and by the Jewish community. So when I get up and announce I'm a lesbian and show I'm knowledgeable and committed to Yiddish culture and Jewish survival at the same time, I diminish some of the shame, and cut through the fear and anger. By showing that I'm a Yiddishist, a Jewish activist, a writer, and a lesbian/feminist activist, I can promote all these things.

The Jewish community needs to deal with its homophobia for political and moral reasons. Jews need political allies, and we should look to gay people, women, the working class, the poor—whoever's excluded from white, middle-class, male-influenced mainstream America. We also have a moral responsibility to support those outside the mainstream because they need our help. That philosophy of joining with people who are powerless is part of my particular Jewish socialist inheritance.

Some Jewish leaders say they can't support gay rights because they're concerned that Jews who are gay don't have children and this causes a further decrease in Jewish population. These leaders pressure Jewish women to have children as a moral obligation. But I know many Jewish women who are so ignorant about

I'm committed to forging a women's link to Yiddish culture. I want female Yiddish writers, intellectuals, and political activists to gain greater recognition and appreciation for their contributions. The visibility of women in *Yiddishkayt* from the past ensures greater participation of Jewish women in the present.

178

Jewish culture that it makes no difference whether they have one child or five—they're not going to pass anything on to the next generation anyway. Ironically, the gay Jewish community is proud and visible. They're committed to being Jewish and yes, many do have children. The critical issue is not that I don't have children but that I have a Jewish identity and a sense of Jewish history and my place in it. That's what I can pass onto the next generation of Jews—whether they're my children or someone else's.

After I returned from a trip to Poland with my mother in 1983, I felt a greater need to act as a link in the chain of Jewish history. I understood how Eastern European Jewish culture has been completely destroyed, and I decided I wanted to do something to preserve it in a conscious and deliberate way. To be a bridge to this part of our past, I had to incorporate more Yiddish language, culture, and Jewish themes into my writing and activism. I want to help others grow to love the Yiddish culture that once flourished and gave so much to Jews and the rest of the world.

I see how American Jews suffer from cultural amnesia. They're looking for something; they're experimenting with ways to live as fully identified, conscious Jews. One way for them to do that is to embrace Yiddish culture. This is particularly hard to do because so many American Jews have given up speaking the language. Still, many people have a passive knowledge of Yiddish—they know more than they think they know. It's important to make that passive knowledge active. That's why I've wanted to teach Yiddish again.

Sometimes the task of trying to connect Jews with their cultural heritage seems overwhelming. Sometimes I get discouraged. But I feel that my own creative survival is linked to the survival of *Yiddishkayt*. So I can't give up on it. Neither can I forget my roots in the lesbian/feminist community. I'm a lesbian/feminist, a Yiddishist, an activist. None of that feels contradictory. I feel integrated. I feel whole.

IRENA KLEPFISZ
Cherry Plain, New York

Atonement

Sometimes I'm in such pain I want to scream. I hold it inside, work on my music, try to find a place to be by myself. When I've felt this way for too long, I break down and cry my eyes out. When my mother comes to visit me here, she cries and then I cry, and that upsets her even more. There's one thing I've learned in here—I can't let my feelings out.

I'll feel guilt for the rest of my life. What I did was a tragedy. It's a sin. I don't know if God forgives me but

Before I was arrested, I was studying at the Mannes School of Music. I still practice on my small electric piano in my cell or in the music room. When I get out, my dream is to play in a piano bar or a pit band on Broadway.

I've never prayed so hard in my life. I talk to God all the time; I ask Him why. Every day I go over the incident in my mind and I try to turn back the clock.

I was selling a couple of pounds of pot and I owed the deceased $1,000. I was going to pay him, but he started making threats against me and my family. I got so scared I grabbed my friend's gun. If I hadn't been high on coke, pot, and booze, I can guarantee that he would still be alive and I wouldn't be in here. But how do you convince a judge that you really didn't expect something like this to happen?

I was nineteen when I was arrested; I'm twenty-three now. That's four years of my life spent behind closed doors—I've done a lot of soul-searching. I know my sentence doesn't make that man live again, but I'm ready to get out and make a life for myself. I don't think it's beneficial for me to sit here any longer.

Prison is certainly not my element. The guards are surprised when I say "please" or "thank you"—some of the other inmates steal their wallets and pick their pockets. When I have a visitor, I always change into a nice ironed shirt, sometimes a tie, and good shoes. The other women make fun of me. They don't understand that I want to look proper.

There are about sixteen other Jewish inmates here. They carry themselves well, they dress well, and I always want to ask them, "What the hell are you doing in the criminal justice system?" You know the stereotype: "What's a nice Jewish girl doing in a place like this?"

My answer to that is, "I've made a mistake." I'm still a nice Jewish girl. I'm not from the streets. I'm no angel, but I'm from a semi-Orthodox kosher home, went to Hebrew school, had a bat mitzvah. My mother spoiled me rotten with the clarinet lessons and piano lessons. I'm still wearing regulation prison pants, though, and I have a number. We're all wards of the state.

FRANCINE GOTTFRIED
Bedford Hills, New York

I often think about writing a letter to the deceased's parents to tell them I'm sorry. My grandmother's way of forgiving me is to say, "He was a drug dealer," but I still can't help thinking that he was somebody's son.

Balance

I'm a TV news camerawoman. In my job, I'm exposed to a lot of the negative side of human interaction. After days filled with murders, abuse, and corrupt politicians, I sometimes lose my perspective on the balance of good and evil in the world.

I've always yearned for a spiritual context in my life. I sometimes went to temple as a child, but I didn't find spiritual or religious fulfillment there. It seemed more like a social ritual. In high school I began to develop a Jewish identity. It seemed to be mostly the Jewish students who had a social conscience and were involved with civil rights. This was something I could identify with and be proud of.

When I went to college, I met people who had never met a Jew before. Some had been taught that Jews had horns. It didn't occur to them that I might be Jewish; I assured them that I was. I didn't like it when people assumed I wasn't Jewish.

The first time that I was in a home when the Sabbath candles were being lit, I felt a deep connection with the ceremony. It was filled with devotion and love and seemed the closest to whatever it was I had been searching for. I've always loved to recite the prayers for blessing the bread and wine and for lighting the Hanukkah candles. Although we did not practice these rituals at home when I was growing up, it felt like it was in my blood, a part of me. But I still don't relate to going to temple, especially here in New York, where you have to make a reservation and pay for a ticket to go to temple on a holiday.

I'm very aware of the contradictions between my personal ideals and the way Judaism is manifested in real life. As a Jew, I'm disappointed and angry with Israel today. I don't think its government is acting in accordance with the Jewish values I was brought up with. Israel should be a place where people work together, not a country that continues to oppress and deprive a people of their homeland in the name of past oppression and suffering of Jews. I can understand how intensely Holocaust survivors might want to create a safe place. I don't want another Holocaust either; but the only way to achieve security and, I feel, the only way to be a responsible and full human being, is to be concerned for the other people on this planet. Our past oppression as Jews does not justify our oppression of others. Jewishness means feeling a connection with all humanity. By that I don't mean assimilation, but rather, a sense of connection.

I find it particularly painful to see Jews acting cruelly to other people. Once I was covering a story about gay rights and I heard some Hasidic men shouting hateful things at the speakers. Their attitudes toward gay men and lesbians reminded me of Nazis speaking of Jews. I wanted to ask them, "Don't you hear what you're saying? Have you forgotten that the same words were used against you, in your lifetime, and now you use those words against others?"

I need to reconcile the negative things that I see around me with my belief that there is ultimate justice in the world. I know that it all balances out in the end. When people are good, good comes back to

I cover stories all the time about rotten landlords. Whenever one of them happens to be Jewish, I feel horrible. I'm angry with them for betraying their Jewish heritage and cheating their tenants. Then I hear anti-Semitic remarks from the people around me. They say, "Oh, another Jewish landlord ripping people off." It's very painful for me, and I don't know how to respond.

them; when people send out negative energy, that comes back to them as well. Some call it heaven and hell, some call it God's judgment, some call it karma; it's all the same thing.

Being Jewish means believing that intellect is something to be developed in a person, but only if the mind is connected to the heart. It's having a social conscience and yearning for justice, knowing that all people deserve our respect. We are here to add to the positive energy of the world.

JANE LURIE
New York, New York

My mother gave my sister and me our political education. She wasn't a member of the Communist party, but she was always on the left. She said that being political was the best and most important part of being Jewish—and being alive.

Messenger

The Lubavitcher Rebbe sent my husband and me to Los Angeles fifteen years ago to work with the Jewish immigrants who had arrived from Russia. When we first moved here, we were aware of how small the Orthodox Jewish community was. It was disappearing; people were losing Judaism. We felt like pioneers.

It was a challenge for me to be in California. I grew up in a sheltered Hasidic *shtetl* in Brooklyn; here, I was suddenly exposed to the rest of the world. California is quite seductive—there are no rules, it's la-la land. I felt I could do and be anything I wanted, nontraditionally, without my mother and grandmother looking over my shoulder. I had to learn how to live in L.A. and still maintain the high religious standards I had in New York.

It is more exciting for me here. In New York I would have been a teacher or a community worker only. I would have restricted myself to the Jewish community. Now, I work in real estate in addition to my work in the Jewish community. When I started studying for my real estate license, a woman—who I think was Jewish—confronted me. "How are you going to remain an Orthodox Jew and sell real estate?" she asked. "Someone will call you on Saturday and say he has a deal—how will you turn it down?"

I laughed and told her that since I don't answer the telephone on Saturday, I wouldn't have a conflict. But more importantly, I would never give up Shabbes just to earn more money. I have my priorities; I know who I am.

Some people say that it is too dangerous for Jews to be exposed to the secular world because it would change them—for the worse. But I don't think that God created the rest of the world as a temptation from which we need to be banned. There are a lot of passing pleasures that we shouldn't—and don't—take part in, but there are a lot of wonders in the world in which we can participate.

I had my colors analyzed, for example, and I found out that I'm especially suited to the color peach. What's wrong with that? Color analysis doesn't affect my religious beliefs—I'm not saying that in another life I was a peach—I'm just having fun with colors. My husband feels that women should do the best we can for ourselves.

It's an open secret that Orthodox women have a lot more freedom than Orthodox men do. I would hate getting up at a certain time every morning to put on *tefillin;* I would resent having to wear a *tallit katan.* I'm not a rigid person. I love the fact that I can study the same things men do, I can pray three times a day as they do, but it isn't an obligation for me.

Most of the commandments that Orthodox Jewish men must fulfill are prescribed by time to increase their awareness that the world was not created randomly; rather, it was made in an orderly fashion by a higher being. Women are freed from these time-bound obligations because our bodies have an innate, intrinsic understanding of the order of the universe; we already have a sense of nature and time.

I feel my life as an Orthodox Jew is a lot richer than the life of an assimilated American Jew. I have tradition, education, and experience, as well as a sense of assurance. I know my children will continue on the same Jewish path, just as I've followed the path of my parents and even my great-great-grandparents.

Here in California, people are searching. One month they discover EST, the next month they try channeling. Some people have compared the Lubavitcher Rebbe to a guru, *l'havdil*—I shouldn't even speak of the two in the same sentence—but he's far from that. He didn't pop up out of a need I have; he'll never be disproved as a fake and suddenly disappear. Before him, there were other great Hebrew sages, including Moses, who guided us. I know our religion has continuity. Judaism will never be a passing trend.

FAYGE ESTULIN
Los Angeles, California

I think it's a cop-out when Jews say that we are just like everybody else. We're not. Jews were chosen to bring the Messiah to this world. That is our task. The way to bring Him sooner, rather than later, is to raise the level of this world from the mundane to the spiritual—even on a fun holiday like Purim. Bringing the Messiah closer is the focus of my life.

Our children know who they are. The first things they learn are blessings over food, not "Mary had a little lamb."

Kaddish

About three years before my father died, I started putting on *tallit* and *tefillin*. I had been trying to say morning prayers before then, but I had a lot of difficulty with the language of the prayers. The masculine, hierarchal, triumphant imagery didn't speak to me. But when I read the prayer that a man says while putting on a *tallit*, I found it beautiful. The prayer conveyed an image of God as sheltering and embracing, and spoke of how putting on the *tallit* is like taking refuge in the shadow of God's wings.

I prayed with a *tallit* for a while, and then I started to think about putting on *tefillin*. Those prayers are also powerful. When you wrap the *tefillin* around your middle finger and forefinger, you say, "I betroth you to me with justice, righteousness, and love." It is as though every morning you marry God.

I went to the local Judaica store, where I bought my *tallit*, to buy *tefillin*. The storeowner—who's very observant—told me, "You have to adjust the knot for the head—what size head does your husband have?" I said, "The same size as mine." I thought if he knew that I would be praying with the *tefillin*, he might have refused to sell them to me.

I don't put on *tallit* and *tefillin* because I want to be like a man. I yearn for the sensation of physical prayer that Jewish men have. I once had a vivid spiritual experience, during which I saw a mother figure who was there to care for me. In her presence, I felt myself opening, changing, developing, and eventually dying. Wearing *tallit* and *tefillin* allows me to reconnect with that imminent, nurturing mother figure. It allows me to feel physically a God who is bound up in my life and embracing me.

Tallit and *tefillin* have helped draw me deeper into Judaism. As a lay chaplain supervisor in a hospital, I feel I work better with people now that I have a greater awareness of my own religious feelings. I often deal with people who are faced with the death of someone they love. I have learned that people who follow elaborate religious mourning rituals are able to move through their grief more easily. I studied Jewish mourning practices and saw the psychological strength they could provide. I sensed that when one of my parents died, I would follow these rituals as a way to help myself.

My father died suddenly when I was forty-three; I was in a daze. Right before the funeral service, the rabbi cut the lapel of my jacket to symbolize the cutting of the fabric of one's life. I was jolted into the realization that my life had been rent apart by the death of my father.

As the garment was being cut, I said a prayer acknowledging that God is the true judge. It was incredibly painful to say that God had judged correctly in my father's death, but it was absolutely essential to the process of grieving. The prayer cut through my denial. Regardless of whether I thought his death was wrong, I had to accept that there is a truth in the divine order of things, and that my father's death was a part of that order.

After the funeral, I followed the ritual of *shivah*, an intense seven days of mourning. People came and brought food, they cooked and cleaned up so that all my energy was devoted to grieving. Visitors told stories about my father; their anecdotes helped me make sense of my father's life and my life with him.

I am committed to *davening* every day for the rest of my life, and yet I am not counted in the *minyan* of my *shul.* It is ironic: A reform temple that would count me in its *minyan* doesn't have daily services in which I could say *kaddish.* Instead, I have to *daven* with ten men who won't count me. Yet I've stuck with Jewish tradition despite the tension because if I went to any other religion, I'd have to give up so many beautiful traditions and rituals.

For the next thirty days, I wore the jacket that the rabbi had torn. I didn't cut my hair, I didn't listen to music or go to parties. When the *sheloshim* period was over, I took off the jacket and put it away. I had a distinct feeling that my grief was beginning to lighten a little.

There is a superstition that the souls of the dead wander around in purgatory for twelve months before they go to heaven. Only really terrible people's souls wander for an entire year; most people are allowed to enter heaven after eleven months. A child is required to say *kaddish*, the mourner's prayer, for those eleven months to help pave the way for a soul's movement into heaven.

It is a traditional obligation for a son to say *kaddish*, but I wanted to say it for my father. I don't believe in the concept of purgatory, but I wanted to say the prayer to honor my father and to have a sacred space to be connected to him every day. I also felt it was a way to honor my tradition, to demonstrate that I was now taking up the mantle of Judaism in my father's place.

Kaddish is a crazy prayer. We have to stand up when we are filled with pain and anger, and talk about how wonderful God is. But during these eleven months, I've felt myself slowly moving from the rage, grief, and despair, to experience the wonderfulness of God and His creation. The prayer never mentions death; it is an affirmation of life.

The other dimension to this prayer is that most people don't know what the words mean. I say it as a chant, almost as a mantra. When I hear the opening sounds, "*Yitgadal v'yitkadash,*" I receive a message that is much larger than the words. The words could be nonsense syllables: In fact, the prayer has a greater emotional impact for me because I don't stop to think about what the words mean.

In modern America, you're not supposed to cry, you have to be strong. But in traditional Jewish culture, crying is accepted and valued. It isn't seen as a sign of pain—it's a sign of healing and recovery. Jews have learned not to be afraid of mourning, perhaps because Jewish history is a continuous cycle of grief and rebirth, death and renewal. The *kaddish* prayer helps us understand this cycle.

Saying *kaddish* helps me reconcile being a fatherless child with being a human who strives for a spiritual relationship with God. Sometimes when I'm *davening*, I'll squeeze the leather *tefillin* strap in my left hand. I feel like I'm squeezing God's hand. God is there with me and I'm not alone.

PHYLLIS TOBACK
Chicago, Illinois

My daughter, Allison, has her own distinctive style and private spirituality. But we've grown closer because we both appreciate each other's inward journeying.

Midrash

Biblical stories contain kernels of the truth of life. The idea that these stories—these *midrashim*—have been passed down for thousands of years convinces me that they are important. While I don't have a traditional allegiance to Judaism, I feel the stories have always been a part of me.

In 1969, I began to study the stories about women in the Bible to include them in my art. I had already begun my involvement in the feminist movement as one of the first eight women in Connecticut to join NOW, and I wanted to examine the historical role of women in Western culture. As an artist, I had already suffered from the limits society imposes on women: People didn't understand how I could be a wife and mother and still want to do my artwork. I was creating my art in a hostile world; there was no serious interest in my work and little encouragement. I felt that the only way to understand my place in the world was to step back and examine how women acted and were treated in the past.

At that time, I was sculpting musical instruments and figures and heads. Then I discovered masks. I felt that the masks I created were a comment, an antidote to the way the female image is distorted in society—by make-up, clothes and attitudes—making it difficult for women to know who they really are. I also liked the idea of people participating actively in my work—not just viewing it from afar.

I decided to make masks of Sarah and Hagar, the first women in the Bible I had studied in depth. Then I began performing their stories in a piece entitled "Mask Ritual Tales," using masks as well as dance, mime, and storytelling. When I put on these masks,

people listened to me. I had learned that society didn't want to hear women bearing witness to their own experiences, and the masks have helped me to artistically overcome that barrier.

In performing these pieces, I treated the women in the Bible as pivotal characters, even if they are not usually considered the focus of the tales. Sarah, for example, was the one who acted to bring forth God's prophecy that Abraham would be the father of the Jewish nation. Abraham had lost faith and was ready to give up—it was Sarah who urged him to have a child with Hagar to fulfill God's promise. I was shocked by how Abraham had treated her before this as well. I couldn't believe that he gave her to the Pharaoh and in exchange (which he no doubt negotiated) received sheep, oxen, gold and silver, male servants and maid servants. It struck me that Sarah—as well as the other women in the Bible—had a real presence, an importance, even though she was phenomenally handicapped by the social structure of her time.

In Sarah's story, the sacrifice of Isaac had the greatest impact on me. Put yourself in her position: a lifetime of yearning for a child, then your husband takes it upon himself to sacrifice your child to God. How can you expect he'll return? What an enormous violation, to have a child whom you have nurtured and preserved taken away from you—and by your husband, to whom you had given your total support! That was Sarah's experience, but her reaction is not even mentioned in the Bible story.

I read between the lines. I can clearly imagine how Sarah felt when she watched her child go. I identify

The tale of Jepthah's daughter is a story of a father sacrificing his daughter. She has no name, no protectors, and, unlike Isaac, she is sacrificed. It's a profound and very sad tale.

with Sarah's pain through my suffering of the death of one of my own children. Having had the joy of bringing children into the world, I also know that losing a child is an intolerable cruelty.

Yet Sarah maintained a powerful belief in God despite all she lived through. I could see divine intervention on her behalf. Her son, Isaac, returned home. He was saved. You might ask me, "What about your life? There was no divine intervention for you—your child died." But there was divine intervention for me, there is a miracle: The very day after my daughter died, my second daughter was born. A healthy, whole child who is now a superb young adult. It's no wonder that I derive strength from Sarah's story. Still, we must remember that this is a tale of betrayal, and of Abraham's willingness to betray her.

I have performed the tales of Sarah, Hagar, and other women in the Bible to thousands of people around the world. Speaking out in a dramatic, highly-charged way in the stylistic frame of the mask tale has been, in part, an exorcism of grief. It has also been a way to apply the ideas, issues, problems, and solutions that confronted biblical women to my own life and to the lives of other women. These stories have a contemporary meaning and message.

My interpretations of the Bible have helped me claim a Jewish heritage for myself. Traditional Judaism doesn't capture me because it doesn't give women enough of a role. Without real equality, the religion can't engage me. On the other hand, by making the women in the Bible visible, I am transforming Judaism so that it encompasses women's experiences.

My "Mask Ritual Tales" are modern *midrash*. The *Midrash* is a collection of tales—some say they were told by women—that embellish and comment upon biblical stories. It's where the real issues in the Bible are hammered out. Each generation uses *midrash* to find new angles—and that's what has kept the Bible alive and relevant for thousands of years. Performing these stories is my *midrash*: a way for me to contribute a female artist's ideas to the Jewish heritage. I give women a place of honor in the Bible and thus I can draw strength from them as well as from Judaism.

SUZANNE BENTON
Ridgefield, Connecticut

I want to uncover our Biblical heritage so that women can learn how our sense of identity evolved. Knowing and facing the truth about the past is a step toward changing our future.

Talmud

For the past fifteen years, I've been studying the Talmud from a feminist perspective. I'm interested in the way the Talmud portrays women, how its legislation has affected women, and the changes that have developed in women's legal status over time. I'm trying to understand what it was like for a woman to live in Talmudic days: What was her relationship with her husband, her father, her children? How much freedom did she have both inside and outside her house?

I live my life very differently from the women of that era. Even though I grew up before the feminist movement, I've always felt I had many options open to me. My parents stressed the importance of doing something with my life in addition to getting married and having children. I can't relate to the subordinate position of women in the Talmud—I am an equal partner with my husband in our marriage, I *daven* in a *shul* that counts women in the *minyan*—but I am fascinated by the Talmud because it gives me a historical perspective on the role of women in Judaism.

The Talmud is a wide-ranging legal and ethical commentary. It is completely unpunctuated—you don't know where the sentences begin and end—and it's written in both Hebrew and Aramaic. It comprises about sixty volumes—thousands of pages—and represents the thinking of rabbis in different countries over a period of five hundred years.

The Talmud was passed down verbally from generation to generation until it was written down in about the seventh century C.E. After that, there were very few additions, but that doesn't mean Judaism has stopped changing since then. My research in Talmud has led me to believe that Judaism, as embodied by the Talmud, is a still-evolving religion.

If we study inheritance laws, for instance, we can see the changes with regard to women that have developed over the years. According to the biblical text, women could not inherit anything from their fathers. Talmudic rabbis felt that this was wrong, so they reinterpreted, they made accommodations. They found a way to limit that law to very narrow circumstances and they devised new legislation. Although women didn't achieve full equality under Jewish inheritance laws until the Middle Ages, talmudic rabbis did improve women's inheritance rights. The arguments and opinions in the Talmud were the vehicles by which rabbis could help Judaism adapt to the times.

This is the beauty of Judaism and the reason why I don't think Judaism is flawed. If we find a Jewish law wrong for today—such as the law that prevents women from initiating a *get*—we can study and learn time-honored techniques of the Talmud and figure out ways to read the law so that it maintains its validity. By immersing ourselves in the Talmud and other ancient Jewish texts, we learn how rabbis of the past devised ways to introduce changes while remaining true to the Jewish legal system. They established a way of interpreting that can be applied to the needs of today.

The talmudic rabbis are my heroes. It's true, they definitely discriminated against women—they were,

I get furious when someone calls the Jewish feminist movement a passing fad. Could you ever suggest that black people wanting equality is a passing fad? It's a social truth. Women deserve to have the same opportunities and options as men, and once you realize that, there's no going back.

after all, influenced by the mores of their days. But they were humane individuals; they expressed their sensitivity by improving women's rights in marriage and divorce laws, inheritance, and financial status. We can mirror their compassion, humanity, and sense of social justice, and apply them to areas they never dreamed of: adapting Jewish laws so that the practice of Judaism becomes totally egalitarian.

Who can change these laws? That is a difficult question. If you asked me who were the leading rabbinic authorities to introduce lasting legislation in the year 200 C.E., I'd be able to tell you. But I don't know today which rabbis will provide answers that will endure through the next century or two. Only time will tell.

Yet it isn't only rabbis who can be involved in this legal process. Jewish women have an exciting opportunity now to study Talmud and to devise their own solutions to problems. If a woman becomes learned enough, other women could go to her with their legal questions; she could act as a *posek*, a decision maker, on Jewish law. It would be wonderful if women engaged other women in finding answers within Jewish law. Great changes—by and for women—could come about that would withstand the course of time. But the only way this can happen is if women become as knowledgeable about Jewish texts as men are.

I've always been interested in studying Judaism. When I went to Jewish camp, I was intensely jealous of kids my age who knew more Hebrew than I did. I always felt I could learn more, study more, observe more. I still believe that Jewish learning continues

through life. If people give up their Jewish education before they achieve complete intellectual sophistication, they will be ill-equipped to analyze Jewish issues maturely. I feel that you have to keep studying to pursue Jewish life in a meaningful way.

While I was an undergraduate at Barnard, I began taking courses at the Jewish Theological Seminary. I received my master's degree, and eventually my Ph.D., in Talmud. During that time, I began to teach at the Seminary's high school; now I teach in the rabbinical school. I might have tried to be a rabbi if the option had been available to me. But I don't feel angry; the route I've taken—learning and studying Talmud exclusively—enriches my life.

I don't think I could pass Judaism on to my children if I hadn't studied the laws so thoroughly. When they ask me why we can't ride on Shabbat, for instance, it's easy for me to cite a code of Jewish law explaining the reasons. I like appealing to a higher authority. But at the same time, I am antifundamentalist. When I study Jewish texts, I use the same critical, scholarly methodology that I apply to secular texts. I am not afraid, for example, to discover that there are two stories of Creation in Genesis. This might raise questions about the divine origins of the text, but studying Talmud openly and critically hasn't made me less of an observant, believing Jew. I have to confront what I see and come to terms with it. I have a passionate commitment to the truth.

JUDITH HAUPTMAN
New York, New York

If you stop your Jewish education before you reach your complete intellectual sophistication, then you will think about your secular issues in a sophisticated way, but you'll analyze Jewish topics immaturely. The only way to pursue a meaningful Jewish life is to keep studying.

Renewal

I don't talk to many people about the *mikvah*, the ritual bath; it's hard to describe the ritual in a word or two. People assume that it's related to a blood taboo and that it implies that women somehow become dirty when they menstruate. I see the *mikvah* ritual on a much higher spiritual level that transcends any notion of "dirty" and "clean."

The first time I went to the *mikvah* was when I was twenty-one, the day before I was married. My mother never went to a *mikvah*, but my husband is religious and he urged me to go. All I remember is cleaning myself totally, and then the *mikvah* attendant insisted that I wipe the polish off my nails and cut them down. I was upset because I wanted to have polished nails for my wedding. People had told me what to do in the *mikvah*, but no one had explained why.

It wasn't until I traveled around with my husband after we were married that I sensed the *mikvah* has greater meaning than simply a thorough physical cleaning. I visited a *mikvah* next to the House of Love and Prayer—a synagogue for hippies—in San Francisco. The *mikvah* attendant there was a beautiful, observant earth mother who was very excited by the *mikvah*. I thought, if a woman like *that* loves the *mikvah*, there has to be something more to it. The second *mikvah* I visited was in Santa Fe, and the woman there was Hasidic and also very spiritual. After these two experiences, I studied Jewish texts and learned that the *mikvah* ritual is really an affirmation of a woman's femininity and creative potential.

Jewish women like myself, who weren't brought up with the *mikvah* ritual, are in a unique position. We've taken on the obligation by choice, so we have a fresh outlook on the tradition that we can pass on to our children and to other women.

Basically, when a woman has her menstrual period, she is *tumah*. Some authorities translate this to mean ritually impure: When the Temple existed in Jerusalem, a menstruating woman could not enter it. I believe *tumah* is more closely linked to the fact that a menstruating woman has lost the potential fetus inside her; this loss brings her closer to death, puts death inside of her—she is, then, physically impure. After the *mikvah*, she is *taharah*, ritually pure. She is returned to her creative potential; she is able to conceive again. In a sense, she becomes godly. In the past, some Jews translated these terms as clean and unclean—that's why the *mikvah* ritual was seen as some kind of denigrating procedure, an enforced cleansing.

I'm not concerned with the idea that the Bible tells a man who has sex with a menstruating woman that "he'll be cut off from his people." What does concern me is the chance of damaging the potential offspring. There is a strong belief that a child who is conceived when some sense of death remains on the mother is at a spiritual disadvantage. Who knows why some people have great fortune in life while there are others for whom nothing seems to go right? Just as I don't smoke or drink alcohol when I'm pregnant to nurture my genes *physically*, I go to the *mikvah* to nurture my genes *spiritually*.

The *mikvah* ritual dates from biblical times. The Bible says that when a woman gets her period, she is forbidden any intimate physical contact with her husband. After her period ends, she counts seven spotless days and then goes to the *mikvah* after sundown on the seventh day. When I leave the *mikvah*, I feel like I'm reemerging into life. That's why I check to make sure that every part of my body is clean and perfect.

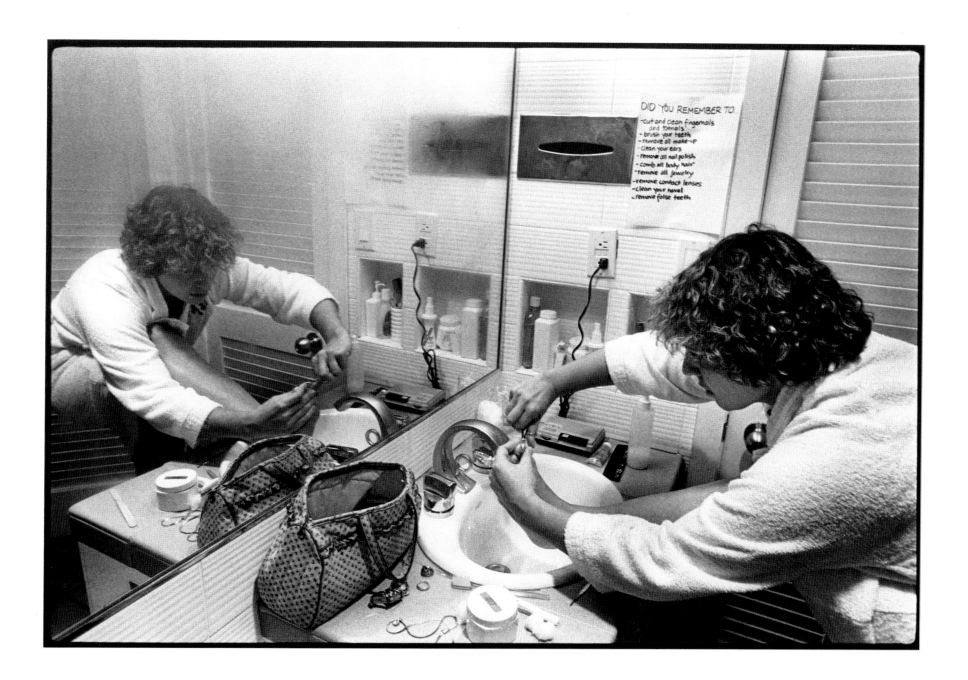

After I bathe, the *mikvah* attendant checks for stray hairs or particles on my body. This insures that the *mikvah* water will touch me everywhere. In the *mikvah*, I feel most closely connected to my Source, to God.

Every *mikvah* must contain running water—sources call it "living waters"—from an underground stream or from the rain. Sometimes after I finish immersing myself in this water, the *mikvah* attendant yells, "Kosher!" I feel like a chicken.

I'm always tremendously excited right before I go to the *mikvah*. I feel tingly all over. You remember how it felt when you had a boyfriend and you anticipated what would happen when you were with him? There was a certain sense about you; you even walked differently. Since my husband and I separate from each other physically during my *tumah* days, I feel as if I'm courting a strange man.

Just before the *mikvah*, you're required to soak in a bathtub. I lie in the tub and daydream about being suspended in water. I imagine a blue or gold light coming out from within me, a glowing cocoon around me, like the feeling of the sack in a womb surrounding a baby. Then I rinse my hair, blow my nose, clean my ears, and wash my bellybutton. Sometimes I even *giggle*.

After soaking in the bathtub and taking a shower, I buzz the *mikvah* lady and she comes with me into the *mikvah* in the adjoining room. Once I'm in the *mikvah*—the bath itself—I want the water to seep into me, into my pores. I dunk three times and say the traditional prayer and then dunk seven more times for the seven days of the week. This is a custom I learned from a friend who studies Jewish mysticism: Seven is the number of God's emanations.

Although I like to concentrate on the spiritual aspects of the ritual, the *mikvah* also provides a powerful way to get in touch with yourself as a woman, to sanctify your body's cycle, as a human being who's part of a universe that has its own cycles. Just as we can celebrate the waxing and waning of the moon, we can celebrate our bodies, not degrade them. I've heard of a *mikvah* where a woman's nails were cut to the quick and filed with Clorox on sandpaper until they became white. I can just picture these crazed ladies with shaved heads concentrating on what's dirty—punishing themselves for being women.

Divine rules are created in totality: They are designed to benefit you, your husband, your offspring. The *mikvah* heightens my physical consciousness and increases my desire for my husband. In fact, I can't think of any drawback to the *mikvah* as I use it—even the part that keeps me away from my husband for twelve days each month. These laws were passed down in a divine way, not written by a group of angry men. Men can be sexists, women can be sexists, but I don't think God is a sexist.

PAMELA STEINBERG
New York, New York

When I'm immersed in the *mikvah*, I feel like I'm in the womb and I'm about to be reborn.

Transformation

The writer Carlos Castaneda said that the spiritual warrior has no personal history. Jewish mystics of the Middle Ages were loath to disclose details of their personal lives. I hesitate to speak about my own life because its complex and controversial aspects can distract from the Jewish issues I prefer to discuss. Just as the woman who wishes to be appreciated for her intelligence rather than merely her physical presence, I want my statements to be heard, and not overshadowed by the details of an unusual life. If someone would like to get to know me, they are welcome to find me in the Southwest. We will go into the mountains on Rosh Hodesh, light a fire, and offer up prayers.

What kind of Jew am I? I live by Torah because its roots in me have defied two decades of my determined effort to uproot them. Once a *kohen*, always a *kohen*. My maternal grandmother and grandfather were both *kohanim*; their blood cries out in me. My paternal grandmother and grandfather perished together in Theresienstadt; their blood cries out in me. I am devoted to *Qabalah*—Jewish mysticism—because it is a jewel I found long ago that still sustains my self-worth as a Jew. My *shul* is in the mountains of New Mexico and, when I travel, in any ocean, forest, or garden I find. For me, Judaism's best offering is the calendar: a plethora of celebrations, a masterpiece of numerical patterns and symbols, an homage to the *Shekhinah*—the divine presence—in her manifestation as Mother Nature.

Religions, like people, have essence and personality. The essence comes first in the form of revelation. These revelations are words brought back to us by the person who has met with God. These words are just the tip of the iceberg, but they contain important spiritual teachings. This essence is the core around which a religion's personality—its laws and customs—forms. We must not lose track of or get disconnected from the essence because it is the experience of God that we need. That experience is the major ingredient in the process of transformation, of spiritual growth.

It seems to me that the essential teaching of Judaism is faith in God. I get this from the first words of the Ten Commandments, the first major Jewish revelation. The words are traditionally translated: "I am the Lord Your God," and I read them as: "I am the Infinite your Source." The sentence continues on conventionally: "Who has taken you out of the land of Egypt from the House of Bondage," which I read as: "Who has taken you out of the earth of confinement from the house of the lost ones." This sentence is about the way of transcendence through YHWH: the Infinite. The remaining nine commandments discuss the way of transformation. The first letter of the first word of the first commandment, "I am," is Aleph, the first letter of the Hebrew alphabet. This letter symbolizes the silent breath of meditation-creation-God. When you take these statements into your inner being, you are moved to build your life on faith in the invisible planes of reality where the Infinite resides.

Why should we practice transformation and transcendence? I am going to quote again from the Torah, but please don't get the idea that I am a conventional academic Jew—I am raising the issues I have thought about and for which I have given myself an-

On the eve of Shavuot, I performed the *mikvah* ritual in the Rio Grande River just like our ancestors did in the Jordan River.

swers. "And you shall be for Me a realm of priests, a holy nation" (Exodus 19:6), and "I will give you as a light to the nations" (Isaiah, 49:6). The Torah's vision for the Jews is that they can generate enough energy to guide others as well as themselves in the process of evolving consciousness.

The question, then, is how to live a full life for oneself and still have energy left over for others. Materialists will tell you that prosperity is the answer; people like myself say that the only way is to learn to recycle negative energy into positive energy, to conserve energy, and finally, to create energy. When I speak of energy, I speak of psychic energy; with psychic energy, we create our realities, the lives we live. And the source of that psychic energy is God. So, we have come full circle. We cannot afford to lose our connection with God, we must constantly prepare for the encounter with God. We never know when it will happen; our time is not always God's time.

How can we invite God's presence in order to have a transformational experience that will bring us to a new level of spiritual awareness and activity? Ritual is one way. Ritual is gesture wedded to intent; sometimes performed in a special place at a special time, sometimes not. Through ritual we participate in the ongoing process of creation; creative ritual generates psychic energy. A good ritual maker taps into a vast body of knowledge on meditation, prayer, healing, the arts, the ways of Mother Earth. Another way is meditation, my life strategy. My needs are aesthetic: I surround myself with beautiful pictures and objects, music, words, and fragrances.

We emerge from the earth and reach for the heavens.

I believe that personal transformation—our growth toward holiness—is the biggest step we can take to hasten the arrival of *Mashiah*—the Messiah—and Her reign of peace and abundance for the planet. Personal transformation is based on sincere effort

and on the wisdom and understanding of persons who have already mastered this process. This hard work involves effort and surrender simultaneously, and has such a cutting edge that I can tolerate it only because I believe in it. I offer the fruits of this work joyously in praise of Creation. There are no personal rewards.

I dream of a community based on the land, a group of people living Torah and *Qabalah*, training ritual makers, proving that priests and priestesses can function as whole human beings. Such a school-community would provide the larger Jewish community with new ideas. Once we had Miriam and her women, the brotherhood of ecstatic prophets, the Qumran and Essene fellowships, the Ba'al Shem Tov and his Hasidim. Twentieth-century America needs a band of hearty and brave souls, a community of spiritual warriors striving for excellence.

In this community, outer goals of service would be balanced by inner goals of individual growth. We could call this work the practice of esoteric Judaism. I prefer to call it the way of the *Shekhinah*. Her song is the voice of esoteric Judaism, she prepares the way for *Mashiah* by grounding us in humility and making us fly in joy. She likes oral transmission, children playing, adults dancing, hands in the soil, blessing the sick, watching the dark light, listening to the voice of silence.

Sometimes as I wait for this community, I get lonely; as I work, I get discouraged. Then, I turn to the souls on the other side, those who have died or who are not yet born. I call on them for strength and inspiration.

Dreams come true.

KETURA ESHEL
Santa Fe, New Mexico

211

Bat Mitzvah

My bat mitzvah was a coming of age ceremony for me. I'm thirty-nine and I'm embarrassed to admit that my bat mitzvah actually made me feel like a woman. I felt like I hadn't grown up until the ceremony. I conquered something I thought was insurmountable; now I feel I can do anything.

I grew up in an Orthodox community where women were excluded from all religious activities. I sat in the balcony of the synagogue while my father sat downstairs. I watched and listened to him talk about the Torah, but I felt I could never really participate in Judaism. That kind of segregation eventually turned me away from the religion.

It wasn't until I went to an Israeli kibbutz for six months that I saw a different aspect of Judaism. There, Judaism meant being a pioneer, with men and women working and studying together. That was the beginning of my awakening as a feminist. I also saw that there were other ways to be a Jew.

After I was married, my husband and I drove across the United States and ended up in Portland, Oregon. I gave birth to a son and decided that it was time to make our home more of a Jewish home. While we were "temple shopping," we heard about a *havurah*. We hesitated because we thought it would be too New Age and radical for us, but we were both surprised.

We went to our first service on a Friday night in a little Unitarian Church in which the *havurah* rented space. People were very *heymish*—they came over to talk to us and made us feel as if we were a part of the *davening*. I was struck by the simplicity of the service and how *havurah* members determined the direction of the prayers. I was ready to rediscover Judaism; the *havurah* provided me with a safe place to explore my religion. I could ask questions that I needed to pose without feeling I was just getting dogmatic responses.

Two female cantors who were members of the *havurah* served as role models for me. They showed me that women can read from the Torah and be a significant part of the service. I also saw women having bat mitzvah ceremonies; I was impressed by them, and I decided I wanted to become a bat mitzvah—a daughter of the commandments. But I was intimidated. I knew very little Hebrew, I couldn't carry a tune, and I didn't think I would ever be able to learn all that was required.

When we moved to Seattle, we became involved with a Reform temple. It was bigger than the *havurah*, but the rabbi and cantor encouraged congregants to be active participants. I started studying in a class with other adults who wanted to become a bar or bat mitzvah. I felt it was the way for me to become part and parcel of Judaism, to claim something that I never knew as a child: the feeling that women can be just as much a part of Judaism as men.

My son, Nathan, was studying for his bar mitzvah at the time, and he asked me if I wanted to have mine with him. I was concerned that my bat mitzvah would

Nathan and I went through some tough times studying to become b'nai mitzvah. I didn't think I'd be able to learn all that was required, but Nathan was very patient with me. He taught me with his wisdom.

steal the show from his, but it was very clear that this was what he wanted to do. So, Nathan and I sat at the kitchen table and we learned together. We shared an important experience that we'll remember for the rest of our lives.

The other meaningful aspect of my becoming a bat mitzvah was that both Nathan and I were twinned with a mother and son in the Soviet Union who were unable to celebrate their own bar and bat mitzvah. We wrote to them about the portion of the Torah we were reading, how we felt, and how we were celebrating our ceremony with them in mind. At our ceremony, we lay two *tallitot* in the front of the synagogue to represent their presence. It was bittersweet for me to see those *tallitot* there—I was aware of how much freedom we have and how they do not have the opportunity to make their own religious choices. They may never be freed physically, but I felt that we freed them in a spiritual sense.

I was also able to come to terms with my own spirituality at my bat mitzvah. Before then, I called on God when I suffered emotionally or physically, but I never felt His or Her presence in a positive way. I was aware of the concept that God is in each of us, but I couldn't relate to it personally. At the ceremony, I felt God's presence. God was inside as well as all around me.

I'm grateful that I've found Reform Judaism because otherwise I might have rejected Judaism altogether. I've found a way to be Jewish that doesn't feel restricting to me. I have the spirituality and a sense of tradition, but I'm also allowed to make choices. I can light candles on Friday night the way my mother did, but then I can take my family out to eat at Taco Bell.

Not feeling restricted by Jewish laws has allowed me to find my own spiritual path.

Whether I eat milk and meat together isn't important to me. What is important is that I give my children a feeling for their Jewish heritage, encouraging them to ask questions. The other day, for instance, my daughter asked, "How do you start a tradition?" I thought about how I had a bat mitzvah—something adult women never did until this generation—and I said, "You start a tradition by doing it."

PEARL KLEINBERGER
Seattle, Washington

My husband was very supportive of my decision to become a bat mitzvah. Still, I think it's hard for a man—even if he's a feminist—to understand what it's really like to grow up in a religion that puts women in the back seat.

Rosh Hodesh

Rosh Hodesh is the celebration of the new month. Since the Jewish calendar follows the lunar cycle, Rosh Hodesh is also the celebration of the new moon. The monthly holiday has traditionally been a woman's celebration. Women are not supposed to work full force on that day—we're supposed to have some time off.

Jews don't have much information about how women in the past celebrated Rosh Hodesh, but I have come to believe that the holiday celebration revolved around women's menstrual cycles. In the past, women tended to bleed according to the cycle of the moon because their body rhythms were more connected to the rhythms of nature. Since the women also lived communally, they probably menstruated at the same time. My theory is that when their menstrual cycles began—at Rosh Hodesh—they separated themselves from the rest of society (the way Ethiopian Jewish women still do today) and took care of one another. It's likely that they performed healing and other rituals together for a few days. Then they would rejoin the men and ovulate at full moon.

Today, women throughout the country are reclaiming Rosh Hodesh as our own ancient heritage, creating our own rituals for the holiday that encompass the concerns and realities of our lives. Since there is no prescribed written ritual or liturgy for Rosh Hodesh, we use our imaginations and express ourselves spiritually in exciting new ways.

I am part of a community of women that meets every month to celebrate Rosh Hodesh as well as other holidays and life-cycle events, such as baby-naming ceremonies. On the evening of Rosh Hodesh, we usually spend an hour *shmoozing*, then someone leads a discussion about a current social, feminist or religious issue. Then we perform a ritual. Each month, a woman volunteers to create and lead a ritual using her imagination or from Jewish or feminist sources. For example, one month each woman sat in the middle of a circle and the other women gave her a blessing for the new month. Another time, we lit candles to symbolize physical light as well as spiritual light. At the same time, we appreciate how darkness represents the unconscious, protectiveness, and mystery. We've said blessings at the beginning of the winter month of Kislev, for example, to honor this balance of light and dark.

Rosh Hodesh is just one aspect of what I call women's entry into Judaism. In my studies at the Reconstructionist Rabbinical College, I examine Jewish texts and try to find the matriarchal roots of our tradition to guide us. Although most of these texts are male dominated, they are some of the few tools we have to piece together what Jewish women were doing in the past.

I studied a medieval text, for instance, in which the male author talked about a childbirth ritual women practiced in his time. There's almost nothing written about childbirth in Jewish texts. (You can imagine how many rituals there would be if men had babies!) In his text, the author admonished women against performing this ritual, but at the same time, he described the ritual in detail, explaining how women cast circles around a woman in labor. The ritual was fascinating to me. When I gave birth to my daughter, the women from my community were with me in the labor room. They cast circles around me to protect the baby and me during delivery, and then performed all sorts of rituals to welcome Rosie into the world.

Some people in the mainstream Jewish community object to what I do; they contend that I don't have the authority to create new Jewish rituals and traditions. But who gave Hillel the power? Who gave it to Rashi? They took it upon themselves. We earn the right to work for Jewish renewal when we engage ourselves in the Jewish process of studying, learning, and teaching. Women shouldn't wait for a rabbi's permission to create new rituals. We need to take ourselves seriously, empower ourselves, and recreate a Jewish heritage that includes women fully.

Like all of the world's religions, Judaism began as a patriarchy; but I'm not interested in abandoning Judaism to start a goddess religion. I'm a Jew. I want my heritage, but I don't want the patriarchal tradition to continue to speak for me. I feel it's my turn now as a Jewish woman to create the future of Judaism.

JULIE GREENBERG
Philadelphia, Pennsylvania

The point of ritual is connection. Ritual reminds us of our connection to the earth and to the higher power within and between us.

Return

My parents gave me the feeling that being Jewish was like being a member of a great club. Freud was Jewish! Einstein was Jewish! All the talented people on the Ed Sullivan show—except the Beatles—were Jewish! My understanding of what it meant to be a Jew was basic: There were few of us, there were many who disliked us, and somehow we were a gamble in history. We had won despite the odds against us.

Our house felt very Jewish. There was always food and newspapers and people talking loudly, visitors arguing, throwing Yiddish words around the kitchen table. We weren't kosher, but we didn't eat food that was *goyish*. Pork chops were *goyish*, a glass of milk with meat was *goyish*, but a cheeseburger was American and okay.

My mother talked a lot about the Holocaust. Neither she nor my father lost any close relatives in the war, but she always told my sister and me that part of the Jewish family was destroyed and that we should never forget what happened. It seemed to be a miracle that any Jews were still alive. My life seemed very precious: It was as if, somehow, twelve years after the war ended, in a Long Island *shtetl*, I rose up out of the ashes.

My mother also gave me an awareness of what it meant to be a Jew *and* a woman. We talked about how the media made it acceptable—even chic—for men to be Jewish (and marry non-Jewish women) while Jewish women were objects of ridicule. I became angry that other Jews reduced Jewish women

to stereotypes and I started writing about how Jewish women were portrayed in films while I was in high school.

My Jewishness was social and political, but I felt no spiritual Jewish connection. We celebrated Hanukkah, Passover, and the High Holidays—one of my favorite times was walking to temple with my father—but I wanted to do more. Rituals seemed magical. I occasionally lit Friday night candles and attended various synagogues on my own, but I never found a community, nor a way to observe Judaism, that felt right for me. Still, when I began working as a freelance journalist, I found myself drawn again and again to Jewish—and women's—subjects.

When my husband and I went to Bali for our honeymoon, we were invited to a festival in a Hindu temple. Everyone—including us—wore beautiful sarongs; the women—excluding me—carried sacrificial fruits in platters on their heads; incense was burning, drums were beating. This ritual was indeed magical, and I was moved by the Balinese people's sense of spirituality, tradition, and community. Despite my positive Jewish identity, I didn't think I'd be able to find a synthesis of those three values within a Jewish context.

A little while after returning to New York, I began working on an article about people who were teaching Jewish mysticism. I interviewed a rabbi who then introduced my husband and me to a couple who attended an Orthodox synagogue nearby. I had never met Orthodox Jews to whom I could relate, but here were interesting, involved, professional, and spiritual

I am trying to recreate the loving environment I felt when I was growing up. I'd also like to give my children a belief in God—a power greater than themselves that they can turn to in joy and in sorrow.

people who even had a sense of humor! Alan and I attended the synagogue's "beginners' *minyan*," a service for people like me who thought there was a Torah and a "Half-Torah" (rather than a *Haftorah*), and we returned weekly.

The *shul* appealed to us. People whom we had just met invited us to their homes for lunch. We sang songs, we joked, and we talked about Jewish issues and rituals I had never heard about, such as the yearly prayer for rain. I began to feel part of a committed, supportive community. I also appreciated Shabbat—one day each week when I couldn't work, make phone calls, or do errands. Club Med advertises itself as the "antidote to civilization," and that's what Shabbat is for me. It's a time for me to stop *doing* and concentrate on just *being*.

Gradually, Alan and I started observing more and more within Judaism. At first, when we discussed *kashering* our home, Alan claimed that he was going to hang his Italian sausages out the window. I wanted to do everything at once but my husband—who's far less impetuous—convinced me not to rush into it. We studied, we spoke to people, and we gradually added a spiritual and religious dimension to our lives. Since Jews who become more observant as adults are called *ba'alei teshuvah*, Alan and I joke that we are "Bali *teshuvah*."

But the issue of women! A friend once told me that in Judaism everyone has one Achilles' heel to struggle with. Alan misses exotic meals when he travels, for example. For me, it's the conflict I feel being both an Orthodox Jew and a woman. Keeping kosher gives Alan a sense of spiritual discipline, but praying in the balcony of a synagogue—like a fixture or like an angel—gives me nothing. Since I had a bat mitzvah in a Reform temple and did everything that boys did, I can't just sit and observe what the men are doing. At the same time, now that I've felt what seems like authentic Jewish spirituality, I'm not attracted to a Reform temple where I don't feel the same sense of community and tradition.

Until now, I've resolved this conflict—somewhat—by being active in women's prayer groups. It still bothers me that women who want to pray together in a synagogue are obliged to ask men for permission—we should simply form our own *shul* like men do!—but I hope that praying with other women in an Orthodox setting is one way for me to feel satisfied both as a woman and as a Jew.

Being an observant Jew distinguishes me from other Americans. I might be similar to other women who balance a career with a family, but my life has a spiritual purpose. I work hard, I am a volunteer in many different organizations, and even roller-skate through the streets of New York, but Judaism elevates my existence. I've had children because as a Jew living after the Holocaust, I feel it's imperative to bring about new life. I've given them obviously Jewish names—Solomon and Ari—and I speak Yiddish to them. My parents joked in Yiddish and spoke it when they didn't want us to understand, but I've decided to speak Yiddish to my kids all the time. I've come to understand that the language is a treasure filled with humor, insights, and philosophy that I want to pass on.

I try to combine the strength I've garnered as a woman, the independence of thought I've learned as an American, and my deep Jewish convictions. These three principles guide my life.

DIANA BLETTER
Great Neck, New York

Journey

I hated being Jewish when I was growing up. I lived in a Jewish town where the people seemed to have narrow interests and appeared very materialistic. When someone asked me where I was from or if I was Jewish, I was embarrassed. I had a stereotype in my mind about what being Jewish meant, and saying I was Jewish was like saying yes, I am that stereotype. I always had close black friends who were like family to me. I envied their connection with their ancestors and their past. Although I was interested in my grandparents' Russian and Austrian backgrounds, I didn't feel any sense of pride. I felt I had no ethnic identity. Being American didn't give me a feeling of ethnicity, and being Jewish wasn't positive for me. I would have preferred to be black because my black friends had a strong sense of relating to one another in a familial way. I wanted to feel the same bond to a people.

I began working as a free-lance photographer and traveled often. On one trip to Europe, I decided to visit a concentration camp in Germany. I had such ambiguous feelings about being Jewish that I wanted to go there to see what I might find. Going to Dachau certainly opened my eyes. I kept taking pictures of the place and then when I saw a woman crying, I stopped. I tried to imagine what it was like to feel what she was feeling. I wanted to identify with her as a Jew rather than just as an observer. I began to understand that prejudice against Jews in other parts of the world goes far beyond the stereotypes I had encountered on Long Island.

In 1983, I asked a friend if he knew any writers with whom I could discuss story ideas. He told me he knew of one journalist who wrote stories about Jew-ish subjects. I said, "Forget it." The last thing in the world I wanted to do was a Jewish project. I had become more accepting of my Jewishness in a personal way, but I wasn't ready to make a public statement about it.

I met with the writer anyway. She started to tell me about the *mikvah* ritual, something I had never heard of. I couldn't believe that women were following a ritual that seemed based on some ancient idea that a woman's menstrual cycle made her impure. But Diana told me that it wasn't only traditional women who were going to the *mikvah;* there were feminist women observing the ritual as well. We decided to do a story about feminist interpretations of traditional Jewish rituals.

I wanted to learn more about Judaism, yet at the start, I hesitated to say I was working on a Jewish book. I thought I'd be typecast as a New York Jew or an involved Jew. Being interested in the religion evoked another negative image. I was also afraid I might be influenced to become more religious or get too caught up in my Jewishness. I thought the project might change me in a way I didn't want to be changed.

The project did change me, but in a positive way. Working on the book has given me my Jewish education; I've learned about my own history. It's been an interesting process to watch how my negative feelings about being Jewish have dissipated.

The project confirmed that I don't have the need to be religious. I went through a short period of experimenting with some Jewish observances. I went to synagogue on Yom Kippur, for example, because I wanted to, not because I felt obligated to, but the services didn't touch me. I've always believed that we're all part of the same source, which can be called God. But I don't need organized religion to give me that feeling of spirituality. I feel I fulfill my spiritual needs through my own prayer and meditation. I have gained a greater appreciation for Jewish rituals and traditions, however. I don't know if I'd ever light Friday night candles or say *kaddish*, but I did start saying a little Hebrew prayer during take-off and landings on airplane flights. But that's the only Jewish prayer I say.

Seeing America through the eyes of Jewish women has given me a new and different perspective. I felt a sisterhood with these women, no matter where I was—in Vega, Texas, or Boston, Massachusetts. Women whose lifestyles, values, and religious beliefs are completely different from my own welcomed me into their homes and I felt genuinely accepted. I think this really was because we were Jewish—we had an immediate rapport. I was very surprised and it reminded me of the connection that I witnessed among my black friends.

My idea of who is a Jew is now quite different from my childhood beliefs. Until I started this project, I did everything I could to avoid being labeled a Jew or a JAP. I believed in the stereotype; I thought Jewish women were overly concerned with their appearance and that they wanted to be taken care of. I often heard women tell their daughters, "You have to marry a doctor or a lawyer." I slowly realized that there are obviously non-Jewish women who have those traits and that many Jewish women around the country have a completely different set of beliefs. I'm no longer bothered by the JAP label on a personal level, but it angers me that people still use the stereotype to define women.

I now feel comfortable as a Jew. There are certain qualities related to being Jewish that I find very positive: a sense of humor, an emphasis on the importance of education, and an awareness of family, heritage, and culture. Judaism isn't a religion or a nationality for me; it's an ethnic group that I'm proud to be part of. Now I joke that I'm glad to be a matzah ball in the melting pot of America.

LORI GRINKER
New York, New York

Growing up on Long Island, I felt like I was just a white American. Although I knew my grandparents were immigrants, they had become rather assimilated. It wasn't until I lived among various ethnic groups in New York City that I really understood what the immigration experience means. I may have had a privileged upbringing, but I now have a greater appreciation of the struggle my grandparents and great-grandparents endured when they arrived in America.

...lgments

...beginning of this project, several people whose ...ledge of Judaism, working partnerships, and women's studies helped us find the path that led to *The Invisible Thread:* Diane Schulder Abrams, Lenore Feldman, Blu Greenberg, Richard Siegel, Sharon Strassfeld, and Jim Weinberg.

For the exhibitions of *The Invisible Thread*, we appreciate the help we received from: David Chalk, The Arts Counsel, Judith Frishman and the Joods Historical Museum in Amsterdam, Norinne Krasnigor, Scott Levinson, Vivian Mann, Andrea Ross, Nancy Rubinger, and Aaron Schindler.

For editing advice and good humor, we extend thanks to Meg Ross; and, of course, we appreciate the work of Marsha Melnick and Susan Meyer of Roundtable Press, who helped bring the book to fruition. At the Jewish Publication Society, we thank Sheila Segal and her staff.

We would also like to thank the women who appear in this book as well as those women we interviewed and photographed who, regrettably, could not be included: Rachel Abrams, Nancy Abramson, Susan Alter, M. J. Bear, Jessie Brilliant, Carla Cohen, Eva Cohen, Basora Eisenberg, the women from the Flatbush Women's Davening Group, Sherry Frank, Tracy Friedman, the patients of Goldwater Hospital, Leslie Goodman-Malamuth, Lynn Gottlieb, Julie Gordon, Julia Hanan, Rivka Haut, Jackie Hershowitz, Susan Isaacs, the women from the Jewish Theological Seminary women's *minyan*, Ariel Katz, Ferdell Lack, Pearl Lebovic, Rose Lahman, Nancy Lieberman, Vicky Littauer, Bess Meyerson, Karen Michaels, Missy Moskowitz, Carol Muldauer, Reut Ness, Amy Persky, Shulamith Rothstein, Judy Sloan, Jeri Soba, Esther the *sheytl*-maker and her clients and employees, Ruchel-Blima Thaler, Sherry Tucker, Carol Walters, the women from the Washington Heights Women's Tefilla Group, Malka Weisenberg, Delores Wilkenfeld, and Clara Zirofski (z"l). They each contributed to our understanding of the invisible thread.

Diana Bletter
Lori Grinker

Many people helped me during the course of this book and I extend thanks to all of them. In particular, I appreciate the encouragement I received from Cynthya Bletter, Gladys Bletter, Hazel Grenidge, and Shirley Singer. I'd like to thank my children, Solomon and Ari Bletter Singer, for putting up with my absences and for their cooperation as I *shlepped* them around—both inside my womb and out. Finally, I thank my husband, Alan Singer, for his laughter, patience, understanding, and love.

D. B.

During the five years I've worked on *The Invisible Thread*, I've learned many things: about patience, about America, about Judaism, and about my role as a photographer. My photography work has evolved and matured through the course of this project. But the most important achievement for me has been gaining an awareness of, and a sensitivity to, the experience of those people whose lives I am interpreting.

Several people helped me gain perspective about these fine points. I owe them a great deal for their invaluable criticism, influence, and professional expertise: Mark Bussell, Charles Grinker, Alain Jullien, Ira Mandelbaum (whose attention to detail in the printing of the photographs went above and beyond what I could ever have expected), Bill Moyers, and Fred Ritchin.

Much gratitude goes to Marc Grinker, Robert Pledge, and Jeffrey Smith, who came through for me at critical moments.

Special appreciation goes to those whose assistance and contributions helped pull together the photographic portion of this book: Tama Bruder, Audrey Grinker, Fred McDarrah, Lois and Stanley Rosenthal, and Scope Associates.

Many, many thanks to all my friends whose love and support is always there for me—whether I'm at home or on the road—and especially to Mark Bobrow, who, in addition to giving much helpful advice, first introduced Diana and me.

L. G.